# *Elephant Juice:*

## Miracles Happen

By

Jeremy McGill

Copyright © 2010
*Jeremy McGill*
New York Church of Christ
37-06 111th Street
Corona, NY 11368

731-608-5716

**HESTER PUBLICATIONS** *Edition*
*www.hesterpublications.com*

ISBN 978-0-9842742-1-5

This Book is
**dedicated**
to three special men:

Kenji, Kyle, Michael 'Sparkie' Smith

"I thank God for each one of you. Your love for your brother will never be forgotten. I learned from of each of you the heart I should have. Know that each of you are in my thoughts and prayers, for only you know the depth of our connection, and I am proud to be your brother and friend, so thank you for being mine."

Sincerely yours, Jeremy

## Acknowledgements

There are so many people that deserve to be acknowledged in the progress of this book and the story that it tells. Some are mentioned in the reading and others are not. I first give thanks to God who saw me through this process. As you will read in notes from the author, this book has taken over two years to complete. Many people worked hard behind the scenes to see to it that I recovered from the elephant attacks that took place in 2008. Ed and Pam Mosby and the church in Spanish Fort, are just a few of the people who jumped into the lion's den with me in order to see my medical needs were met.

Dr. John David Thomas and Burton Williams along with Freed-Hardeman University and West Tennessee Health Care Foundation also saw me through my recovery. The congregations of Henderson, Jacks Creek, and Pinson were also vital to my return to the states, and I owe them along with over 1000's of others a huge thank you, this is one reason I cannot list them all. It would take a book of several hundred pages to do so.

The cover design was inspired by Amber Jo Carwile and Meghan McGehee perfected it with her amazing artistic talents. The photography comes from a lady I truly cherish, Bethany Odom. Bethany has encouraged me the past ten months to finish this book and without her, I do not know if the book would have ever been complete. I need to thank my editors, Nancy Smith, Wade Osburn, and Elizabeth Blythe. Also, recognition needs to be given to Kangseok Kim. Kim has been a true friend and brother since my return from Asia. Kangseok is the designer of my new website http://elephantjuice.us

There are hundreds of other people that should be on here, but I believe the rest of them know who they are, and do not mind if I give all the glory to God. It is because of Him that I live.

## NOTES FROM THE AUTHOR:

Greetings! I am so glad to finally have this work completed for your reading pleasure. I started writing this book nearly two years ago in 2008. It is now September 2010, and I have no idea how successful it will be. To me, just to have it completed is a success of its own. I had no problems writing the beginning because I knew the story line, but like most of my writings the conclusion was just empty, or so I thought. As you read this little story, I pray it brings a deeper connection to the both of us. I want you to know I care about you and look forward to hearing from you in the future. I am easy to reach but not always available because of all the work I am involved in. Nevertheless, if you call, write, or email, I will find the time to reply in one way or another.

I appreciate your interest in my life and the story I am willing to share with you and the entire world. While writing this book, I found myself face down on the ground sobbing as I poured my heart out on paper. I hope your faith is deepened and life reflects truth. I believe God has granted me the gift of teaching and writing, and I believe it is no coincidence you have picked up this book. I usually ruffle some feathers in doing so, but remember it is Christ who calms the sea, and rough waters can be a metaphor for 'all' our lives. Everyone has a story, I just decided to put mine in print, so enjoy the ride and drink the juice, always with love from above, Jeremy McGill.

## Contents:

I. Acknowledgements .................................................. 5
II. "Elephant Juice: The Day I was Buried" ......... 11
III. The Road to China: "Bob" ................................. 21
    "Let's Dance" ................................................. 27
    "Fishers of Men" ........................................... 33
    "Romantic Chains" ........................................ 53
IV. Welcome to China: " Ni' Hao" ......................... 61
    "Kenji" ............................................................ 73
V. Elephant Juice: "Wild Elephant Valley" ........... 87
    "Mercy" ......................................................... 99
    "There's a Stirring" ..................................... 105
    "Suicide" ...................................................... 113
    "I Am, My Brother's Keeper ...................... 121
VI. War; "POW" ..................................................... 133
    "The Battlefield for Freedom" .................... 139
    "A War Within" ........................................... 147
    "Dungeon of Depression ............................. 155
VII. The Road Home: "Love from Above" ............ 161
    "Hope" .......................................................... 171
    "Desperado" ................................................. 177
    "The Enlightenment" ................................... 183
    "God Answers Prayers" ............................... 191
VIII. Concluding Remarks: .................................... 195

# INTRODUCTION:

## *Elephant Juice:*
## *The Day I was Buried*

*January 24$^{th}$ 2008 6 pm'ish Yunan Jungle Southwest China...*

The evening jungle had become curiously quiet, the birds stopped whistling, the crawling creatures stilled by the thundering noises that had just filled the air, even the earth worms had stopped their creeping and crawling motions under the surface of the earth. Monkeys and tree creatures were frozen in curiosity. The only noise was a deep, desperate gasping of air and suffocation coming from my dying body. I looked down at my corpse. I saw my intestines to the left side of my stomach stretching through my blue sport shirt soaked with blood, I felt my entire body was crushed; specifically, my torso had been broken and completely crushed from the inside out. I was only able to maneuver myself, using my right arm to push my broken body into a small dip in the earth. I was like a deer that tries to find that last comforting spot to bleed out after the hunter has struck his arrow.

"So, this is what its like to die," I thought. "Life had finally come to its last fading moments." There to my right were the four giant catalysts of my demise. "What a great way to die," I thought, "but how painful it is to suffer." Just earlier this day, I had experienced an unusual feeling. The feeling was so unusual that I wrote to my uncle Sammy back in Tennessee. I wrote that I loved them and thanked him and Aunt Janet for the comfortable shoes they had sent. I remembered noting "If anything should ever happen to me, just know I love you." Never could I have imagined just hours later I would be here on the earth's canvas gasping for my last breath. My body was completely broken. Lying in a pool of my own blood, I thought about life. Life had truly showed me all of her entities, her love and beauty, her pain and despair, her just and unjust paths, and now with the winds of an ever changing world, it came down to this beautifully pain-staking moment, when soon I would be knocking at heaven's door.

I thought a lot of things in these final minutes. I had been a lover, a brother, a husband, a father, a son, a nephew, a cousin, and most importantly, a friend. And now, I was leaving that all behind, headed toward the greatest venture life has to offer, death and the great unknown. Even though my faith and belief system told me that heaven is my reward, I wondered, "Would this be the case?" As for the afterlife, no-one really knows except those who have gone on before us, and no heavenly light was shining down on me as I had seen in the movies. So maybe, just maybe, I got it all wrong. Maybe, my sins were too great. Maybe, I had not loved with the right kind of love, always placing myself and desires above others. Humbleness and humility were only words I'd liked to have thought I owned.

Thoughts about the funeral that would soon surround the shell that held my spirit began to consume my mind. I saw my mom first. She was dressed in black, wearing a hat and a darkened netted face covering to mask her mourning. I saw my dad still wearing his work uniform, looking on with tremendous pain in his heart, wishing we both had one more fishing trip, a trip to talk about what really mattered in life. And there, amongst them, was my sweet Ally. She had just become my girlfriend a year before. I had tried to love her the best I knew how, and yet, I knew it wasn't enough. I had always loved myself more. She seemed to deserve better than me, and I was always too proud to admit it. Ally was special to me for so many reasons. I was an American redneckish fella, and she was a sophisticated, young, beautiful Russian lady. Not only did she have beauty, but she was also patient with me and sensitive to everything around her. Even there at my funeral she looked like a flower in her yellow dress. Her tears hidden by her urge to comfort others, she would do fine in life without me, but would she know that I truly loved her? Would she know that I had been thinking about buying a diamond ring to place on that special finger? Our relationship, to me, represented so many things, peace being in the center of our togetherness. But, I guess at this point, it really didn't matter. I was dead anyway.

Looking around the funeral, there stood my two heroes, side by side, Granny Margie and Granny Patty. They were dressed as older modest ladies do, one in green and the other in blue. They were holding each other's hands, looking at the box that contained my hollow body. There they sat thinking upon all the memories we had. I can honestly say they might have had a slight grin hidden in their sorrow, a grin that said, "One day I'll see him again and there will be no more tears." My brother Jason and his wife were standing to the left side of my grannies. I didn't tell Jason I loved him enough, and I knew as an older brother I wasn't always loving, but I wished I could have made it up to him some day. And then, to the side of them, my sister. I loved my baby sister, always calling her Nicole the butthole. We didn't get to hang out much, and if I could tell her one thing on this day, I would beg her to love Jesus and to do so with her whole heart. And there behind my immediate family stood a small group of life-long friends looking into the hollow ground that would soon swallow them all.

There on the outside edges were my uncles and aunts, my cousins and high school friends. In and amongst the crowd stood Richard Petty, I bet he was thinking about all those fishing trips we took and ones we always wanted to take. What a great friend he was to me. And there stood Jeff, Mitch, Billy, and JB. I bet these guys were thinking about all the hell raising we had done, and how much fun we had doing it. And then I bet they would reflect on how far we all had actually come and how close we had stayed throughout our lives. And there along with my best guy friends were my high school girls. Jeana, Tiffany, Niki, Ashley, Carrie, Lori and Jenny Smart and Jesse Dale, I sure loved those pretty ladies. If ever people tried to keep me sane, it was these girls. In and amongst the crowd stood my college friends and even a few of the professors who took the time to get to know me. And then all clumped together to the right side were the ones I traveled Europe with. That group of kids had shared a love that forever changed me. They were the lights that led me to know about this being we like to call God. And there's the man who baptized me just two years ago, GL. He stood confident for my soul, and he was also a dear friend. He was also thinking, "One day I will see him again." And, just behind him stood Adam Davis and Bethany Odom. Bethany was quite the humorous lady, and Adam was a little eccentric man but a deep thinker. I was glad Adam and I had become friends, even though sometimes I wanted to kick his butt, him and GL both for that matter, for they often challenged my thinking. And Bethany had always been sweet to me and loved me without judgment.

Glancing deeper into the crowd, I saw some from the local church congregation. They had only known me for a short time, but they greeted me every time with open arms and smiles of grace. There were even a few in the crowd I didn't know, but I'm sure we crossed paths in some way. And those who lingered even further back in the crowd were noticeable, like Mike the beekeeper, the ladies from Wal-Mart, and students from the university who just cared for others. What an amazing sight to have; maybe these thoughts are the visions that inspire Hollywood films, those films that base stories on real life events. It is not that the vision actually happens that a soul soars above the ground looking on at its burial. Yet, it is the mind imagining what it would be like to be at one's own funeral. I guess most would hope their funerals to be a celebration of life, a grand exit from the play we call life, where even though the person was not present, they still stood center of attention, but these thoughts soon faded.

Pain was surging throughout my entire body. I tried to shift to a more comfortable position, but it was not possible. My mind began to think of other possibilities. "Would there come a great, bright light shining from heaven? Would God's voice break through the sky and speak causing me to tremble with fear and to hope for grace? Would his hand grab my head and stick my face into eternal damnation, giving me a glimpse into what grace saved me from?" Desperately, with a low, broken voice, barely able to breathe, I began to pray, "God come. Please come now. It's too much. The pain is unbearable. Whatever my fate, let me meet it now; I don't want to suffer any longer." Turning from this, I began to sing. I sang a hymn I had learned just a few months back. I sang with hope for mercy. The song's lyrics held a hope of what might come. My imagination began to vision how I would like the next minutes to play out. Time, silence, and the smell of death kept hovering over my broken, bloody mush of a body. Thoughts continued to run through my mind in this moment, especially the thought of the afterlife. Suffering in agonizing pain brought me to a point of desperation, and desperate times call for desperate measures.

Death was certain. I was hanging on by thread, and this thread of life that was left, I was prepared to cut and progress into my destiny. Taking my right hand, I placed it on the warm, sensitive, awkwardly, gooey

I placed it on the warm, sensitive, awkwardly, gooey intestines that plunged out of my body in the shape of a small cantaloupe. My thought was, "If God isn't coming to me, I'll just have to go to him." The plan was to grab my intestines and with one fluid, quick jolt, rip them out of the way. The next step would be to take my hand and feel up under my rib cage, grab my heart and disconnect my life's most critical muscle. I felt this was the only way to end the suffering. Now, I only needed the courage to do so.

I closed my eyes, took shallow, sighful breaths. "One, two," I began to count. But hesitation set in. Then, a little more courage filled me as I took a few more deep breaths. I was ready. On the count of three, with one fluid motion and a jerk of my intestines, I would disconnect all that was sustaining my life. I was ready to meet my creator. Now, the courage deepened by the desire to end the pain. "One... two... (deep breath, hand on intestines) and thrre..." Before I could finish the count, I heard a voice of a man, "Hey." I paused. "What's this?" I thought. Looking to my right, I saw that the giants were still just feet away. They could, at any moment come and finish what they had started just moments ago. Yet, despite the possibility of their coming over to finish me off, I tried to holler back to the voice behind the forest walls, but all I could muster up were short, shallow pants. "Hh,... hhh,.... hhhh," I couldn't get any sound to form. I had nearly lost all ability to sound out. Both lungs were collapsed, and I was too damaged. One more time I tried, and with a low, desperate, voice I was able to gander up a sort-of hoot, "Oooh, oooh" came from my mangled body;

a moment of complete silence followed. Then an echo, "Oooh, oooh." Again, I "Ooohed," and again another echo, "Oooh." I looked over and the elephant stared on with their sad eyes, "Oooh, oooh," I murmured, and then another, even closer echo, "Oooh, oooh," then again, "Oooh." The once silenced jungle had came alive with my desperate ooohing cry, and the echo in the wilderness.

As sudden as the voice had come, it faded away. I "Ooohed," but no echo responded. With disappointment sinking in, I tried once more, "Oooh, oooh" and again no echo returned. "Well," I thought, "at least someone knows I'm here. Maybe nothing will come along and eat me before the jungle dwellers find me." I had envisioned a black panther coming along and feasting on my innards, then dragging what was left of my corpse back to her cubs, and after they were finished, the insects would devour the rest of my flesh, leaving only a sac of bones, that may never be found.

I wondered with great thought, "What had happened to the voice in the wild? Did he travel further than my voice could reach, or did he come close enough to see the danger of my presence?" I guessed the latter and drifted off back into my imagination. I began thinking about my body and how it would be boxed up and shipped back to the U.S. and how maybe my death would cause a rippling affect of spirituality among my friends and family. Maybe, my mah' would become a Christian and my dad and sister would follow. Maybe losing me would allow them to think deeper and do some honest soul searching. If so, my life was worth its death. After all, the death of my daughter Laila Lynn eight years prior had led me to deeper thoughts on God and grace. My thoughts drifted from one scenario to another.

I began thinking on all that had occurred in my lifetime. I felt that to leave this day would be to leave in a superior, adventurist manner. I had been a lot of places in life and done a lot of things in my thirty some-odd years. Climbing mountains in storms, skydiving, taking walkabouts in places like Greece, Rome, France, Holland and other European countries were some of the memories that were stirring in my mind. I had hitch-hiked across the U.S. for 29 days once upon a time and authored a book on the journey. I had lived in America's last frontier of Alaska for an entire summer. I had served as an educator in a Chinese university; I served missions larger than my own life's mission. I had always been loyal to my friends, and that might be the one thing I got right. I had seen a great portion of the world. I held many great moments in my heart and had let the bitter ones teach me the lessons we all ought to have the pleasure of experiencing. But some of those lessons, I realized, didn't always take. Truly to die this day would be beautiful, and as for life in general, I was satisfied.

Then, as I looked to my right, I noticed the beasts walking even further away. And out of the darkening jungle the voice once again came, "Oooh, oooh." And with this last hope of being found and with all I had and all I could gander up, I let out a yelp, "Oooh! Oooh! Oooh! Help! Help! Help! Help! Oooh! Help! Help! Help! Oooh! Help! Help! Help!" I didn't care at that moment if the man found me or the beasts were startled enough to come back and finish me off. All I knew was something had to happen... But here, right here in the midst of this moment of extreme chaos and agony, at the climax of my life's journey, I had to ask myself, as many of you probably have, "How did I get here? And what in the world was I doing in the jungle where wild elephants roamed?" It's actually quite a story, and in order for me to explain this to you, my dear reader, I must take you back to the Fall of 2004. Later in the book, I'll bring you back here to the place where God's miraculous hand found me lying in a pool of bleeding desperation. It was there in my weakest moment, that I was given my greatest strength. Thank you for opening this book; I hope to inspire you all. I hope after reading this short story, you dig into your souls and find that divine love that brought me from death back to life. So, with this said, friends, I welcome you to the show. With love, respect, and gratitude, I am sincerely delighted to be a part of your life, and as always, I send you my love from above.

Jeremy McGill

## *The Road to China: Bob*

Fall 2004 Arkansas: World Missions' Workshop... Curiosity brought me into this setting. I had just started a Masters in Education program over at the university in Henderson, Tn. But, it would be here at the Arkansas university that I would find my Asian connections. Before this point, I received a degree in history from a strict, private Christian school in West Tennessee, Freed-Hardeman University. I had taken numerous Bible classes and sometimes private Bible classes. Still though, I had not accepted the Christian doctrine. I did not want to commit to something I knew I would fail at. I knew somewhere in the Bible the man 'they' called Jesus asked His followers to "be perfect," an impossible task, I thought, and one I knew I would never complete. So, "Why try?" That was my philosophy, and I was sticking to it.

Nevertheless, under the guise of a "so-called" Christian from a Christian university, I knew two things for sure: I liked history, and I loved to travel. My degree and my school in this respect could help me reach some of the lands of the ancient East, and there I could put another thumbtack in my global map and another chip on my shoulder. More memories and stories would be created and shared with people in my life. I was especially looking forward to impressing future students with my adventurist tales. And it was right there in Arkansas that I would find the bridge to carry me off to some of the places I wanted to discover. The lecturer this hour was going to talk about the mission work in China for Christian teachers; he began telling a story about a guy he called Bob. And it went something like this...

Bob was a student of his, and throughout the year Bob would come over to his apartment to practice English. Bob noticed a Bible sitting on the table every time he came to the teacher's home. Bob had not really thought much about the teacher's beliefs; I suspect he just knew that something was especially interesting about his teacher, who always seemed happy and smiling, gentle and loving, and interested in Bob's life. Over the semester, the pupil and the teacher came to have a great relationship. Time and time again the student told his teacher he wasn't interested in reading any of the Bible. Yet, he continued to come and practice his English two to three times a week. As time went by and the close of the semester was drawing near, the two knew they would be saddened by the distance that would grow between them. The teacher felt somewhat a failure, for Bob never wanted to study the Bible with him.

The day came when the two would have to say goodbye and go their separate ways: the teacher returning to the U.S. and the pupil finishing his college courses in China. The teacher had begun boxing up his belongings and Bob was there to assist and see him off. As Bob watched the different things being boxed up, he saw that strange book his teacher had asked him to read several times, but he had refused. This time it was being placed inside a box, and it may very well be the last time Bob would have a chance to read it. Bob stared at the book with great intensity in his face. The teacher looked at Bob and said, "Bob, you can have it if you'd like." "Yes!" he replied. So, the book was now the teacher's gift to Bob. "Maybe," the teacher thought, "Bob would read it through and find truth, but probably not, since he wasn't going to be there to help him understand what each verse meant." Aren't we all guilty of this to some degree, arrogance in thinking we have all the answers and that we are right in the way we think? We stand guilty of labeling others as 'they' or 'them' people. We judge without mercy. Truth is, God's word is sharper than a two edged sword, and when one is seeking truth God opens doors. He pierces our hearts with truth and love, He shows us His grace and love, a love none can comprehend.

Eventually, the two went their separate ways. A couple years or so had passed by, and the teacher began to miss China so much that he decided he would return for a second term. He lined things up and thought about Bob frequently. With all things in order, he was anxious and ready to return to his old university in China. This time he knew what to expect and was more anxious than ever to find Bob. Upon his arrival the semester had started and the days were as nonchalant as every day before, and after a few weeks he began to wonder if Bob would ever enter his life again, until one day when a knock on the door came. When he opened his door there stood Bob, with a radiant glow about him and a huge smile. Bob floated into the apartment, and in his hand was the same old, worn-out Bible the teacher had given him years ago. The teacher could tell the book was being used. It was limp and worn on the outside. As the two embraced, Bob looked his teacher in the eye, and with a tear rolling down his cheek in the cutest sincere Chinese accent said, "Teacher, I read this whole book! It is so great that Jesus alive. He has changed my life forever I do believe in the God now. Before you left, I thought the God was just an American God. But, I know now it is for everyone, even Chinese."

The teacher in amazement and awe said, "Bob, you really believe?" Bob's reply brought tears to the teacher's eyes, and not only to the teacher but to everyone in the lecture hall that day. "Yes! Yes! I believe, and so does my father and my mother and the rest of my family. We have all been baptized in the water and believe, and now we live as Christians in the Bible." The two hugged and the teacher knew then that if this were the last time he was able to visit China, the work God had done through him was the most rewarding work of all his life.

As I exited the classroom, I knew I did not want to go to any other workshops that day; China was the place I wanted to be. The world's oldest civilization was waiting to be honored with my presence, such a humble thought I had. I was excited and went ahead and searched out all the literature I could on teaching in China. My heart was pricked as it was back in 2003, when I got stuck on that airplane with those twenty-eight Christians headed to Europe. I had thought going to church and sitting in on Wednesday nights was good enough for my walk with God, and as long as the Christian world thought I was a

Christian, I could run in all their theological circles. And God and Jesus were the crutch that allowed me to do so. If it weren't for the commitment part, I may have even considered being baptized that day, but if I were going to be honest with myself and God, I knew there was no way that this sin-driven man would ever make such a bold commitment to a life that would ultimately end up filled with hypocrisy.

After exiting the class that day, I went fishing with my dear friend Nolan. The last time I saw this fella I had been talking about hitch-hiking across America and about going up to Alaska. Nolan believed in me. He was always cheerful and encouraging. And it was in talking to him that my past comments about the hitch-hiking around the U.S. became a real notion. It was a very spiritual day. After hearing the story about Bob, I found myself standing waste deep in the cool crisp Arkansas stream. The yellow leaves were falling on the surface of the smooth flowing stream, and Nolan and I were reeling in the rainbow trout. I had just heard a very enchanting conversion story. And now, now was the time to put thought into action. The coming summer may just work out for my Hitch-hiking trip. And possibly Alaska wasn't out of reach. Then, I could very possibly go over into China. The sky was the limit, and the stars were within reach. I was at an all time high. I just had to put it all into play. And when I told Nolan my plans, he just gleamed with a smile on his face and said "McGill, you can do anything man." And that's all the encouragement I needed, "Thanks Nolan."

## *The Road to China: Let's Dance*

The days passed by slowly that fall, and it seemed like forever before I would be able to grow my wings and fly away, but soon enough the year ended, and a new year was born. 2005 was a spiritually awakening year for me. Sometimes, I think it would be nice to have a plan and to know that it would work out just as I see it in my head, but then again, that would take all the excitement out of life. So, it was now New Years. Bright, colorful booms filled the night skies, as I sat in another drunken stupor, in a dark bar room, wondering what would come of the New Year. I knew I had been toying with the idea of seeing my country by way of hitch-hiking. There was something romantic about drifting with my thumb in the wind, just blowing about like a tumbleweed, but I kept the idea buried. Finally, summer was near and I decided to go a little crazy.

All my running around painting the towns red had caught up with me, and something new had occurred in my life. Suddenly, I seemed to have a conscience. I was attending church on Wednesday nights, truly wanting to give into God's calling, or at least wanting to want to, but at the same time I was fighting the call with wild parties and loose women. Yet, through a few special mentors and friends of the Christian faith, God was watering the seed planted long ago by my grandmother. Some would challenge my faith as I saw it fit, and others just loved me the way Christians ought to love others. The madness in my mind had to be brought to surface, and in order to deal with my inner demons, a little insanity had to be spewed onto the ones I loved. Eventually, the internal war landed me on the side of the hot July pavement hitch-hiking across the country.

The trip was intriguing enough that I wrote my first book titled *American Hitch-Hiker: Searching for God with My Thumb in the Wind*. Since those days, however, I've come to realize that searching for God is naïve. What really happens is that God is searching for us. God has searched for man's heart since the time Adam and Eve first fell from grace, hiding themselves in the bushes from Yahweh as he walked in the garden searching them out. 'He' came looking for them, and this hasn't changed at all. In fact, He is continuously looking for all of us. Even when we think we have found Him, he still wants more. In fact, He wants all of us. And I hope before the end of this book, you want more of Him. Our greatest moments do come in our weakest hours. And it's when we stretch out our arms in desperation and say, "Father, please father, rescue me," that He holds out his mighty, loving hand, lifting us from the drowning waters and says, "My child, if only you had faith the size of a mustard seed, we could dance on the oceans together." And with this thought, I hope you see that truly walking with God is much like dancing; it's just better when we let him take the lead.

After the summer hitch-hiking trip, I was ready to proclaim my faith in America and even give a little more faith to God. I started another school year and was working on my first book; my next venture was already fresh on my mind. I wanted to see Alaska, and it was possible by the next summer that I could head off again. I just needed to focus and believe. This was a very trying time of my life. I had fallen in and out of love with several different ladies there in the college, but lightning did strike one day. A sweet smile and voice crept out behind a computer in the library one night. The funny thing about that lightening strike is that the thunder wouldn't be heard for years to come. I was dating a few ladies at this time, or at least I was caught up with the whole Samantha romance some of you read about in the previous book, but like a robot mesmerized by his creator, I walked and approached this young, attractive lady in the university library, and with a half cocked-grin and all the wrong intentions, I brought myself to say, "Hello."

Sitting there amongst the rest of the students in the computer lab was the cute, little, finely-dressed lady. She turned and, with a light Russian accent, replied, "Hello." Conversation ensued, and in the conversation a strikingly sad comment was made. She stated she liked America but was not having any fun here at the school, especially because Henderson was such a small town and she was a big city girl. I admit for city slickers Henderson may be the last place they would find a ton of fun; however, I answered her cry for fun with arrogant confidence, "Lady, you're just hanging around all the wrong people. Come with me and I'll show you some fun out on the town." She hesitated, smiled, thought deeply. "Well my American parents may not let me." "Are you kidding me? You're in America now. Freedom is the essence of our people. I'm sure whoever they are, they will let you come along with me; I'm not a bad guy or anything. Where will you be going to church tonight? I will introduce myself to them." Later that evening after meeting the 'American' parents, I was able to convince them to let this beautiful lady join me for a short outing. I explained who I was and that my intentions were merely friendly. Ally's American parents granted my wish.

The next evening, I took young Ally out. We didn't do much, driving around and chatting, sharing a glass of wine served in plastic cups. The conversation was casual at best and soon her curfew came upon us. I felt like a child needing to get her home before midnight, but it was the respectable thing to do, and I gave my word to her elderly American family. I was used to loose women with no regard to rules and regulations. I wondered if Ally would ever grace me again with her presence. However, for this time in life I felt certain I would not be seeing her any time soon. I had called her a few times, but after a while, I could tell she was uncomfortable about hanging out with me. Many questions ran through my mind. Were the American parents opposed to my lifestyle, had she rejected my sincere invitation to a friendship due to the cultural differences, or was I just not good enough? Had there been some back-biting by people who knew I wasn't within the Christian fold as they saw fit? I felt the latter was the most likely scenario. Well, time went by and life continued on. She had disappeared from my sight, but I often wondered what happened to the sad little Russian lady. Even so, I went on chasing all the wrong ladies in all the wrong places. Every now and again the thought of Ally and what ever happened with her life would cross my mind, but it, like all memories, faded.

The Year 2005 soon left as all the other years seemed to leave, full of memories and unfulfilled dreams. 2006 had quickly come into play. My adventurist heart was once again pounded by an unsettled feeling of stagnation, my spiritual walk a wide path of uncertainty and turmoil, and again I would put God to the test. My focus would come back to the waters. Inspired by the fishing markets of the Alaskan fisheries and a wealth of student loan dept created over the past 5 years, I decided now was the time to run off to Alaska and seek a position as a deckhand on a fishing vessel. I, Jeremy McGill, would take on the sea with a dozen others and conquer yet another quest for fame and fortune. Surely, if God loved me, he would rise in the stormy sea and show himself walking across the waters, as he had done for others in the past, and besides, I felt especially intrigued to dare him to do so. If, in fact He would come and show His presence to the storm tossed vessel of my mind, I would turn my life over to Him fully. That was the silent challenge I dared Him to act on.

The summer of 2006 soon approached. My Biblical knowledge had increased. I knew truth, but I was not ready to let the truth grasp me. I liked being free from the thought of being a servant to anyone or anything, especially an authoritarian figure that sometimes seemed unjust. After all, I couldn't see how anyone who loved

His children would let a snake in a garden bite death into His children's veins. Nor, did I think it was very fair what happened to Job. He seemed to be a pawn in God and Lucifer's game of good verses evil. And moreover, how could God forgive such people as Jeffrey Dahmer and other vicious murderers and rapists? It just didn't make sense. Then again, we all have to remember David, of the Old Testament. He killed one of his own soldiers in order to sleep with the soldier's wife, and David was and still is portrayed as a man after God's own heart. I figured if the 'big guy upstairs' let David slide for his acts of desire, surely I would be alright. Yet, this reasoning never settled well within me, and one more time I wanted to put God to the test. For a while, I had viewed various fishing shows of Alaska on television, and that's what I decided I should do.

In my mind, I saw myself and a dozen others out at sea, late nights of drifting for the catch, huge overbearing waves tossing us about, a camaraderie like no other, and a deep bond built in storms and lantern lit nights. Not only would the summer be a great fishing venture, but it would pay well also. And so with three-hundred dollars and a flight to Anchorage, I would soon be off to the last frontier. Life at this point had some disappointments, but through my travels and my education, I was able to hold my head high. No place would conquer my spirit. I packed one bag and was soon to land on the greatest landscape ever viewed by man's eye, Alaska. Little did I know, God and I were dancing, and He was leading the way.

## *The Road to China: Fishers of Men*

I thought I had it all figured out. I purchased a one way ticket to Anchorage and soon my pockets would overflow with money from the fishing success I would have. As my mind's eye envisioned the trip, I would hop off the plane, stroll down to the docks, and offer a helping hand. Within just a matter of days, I would be hired on, and out to sea I would sail. I would become the greatest deckhand fisherman the crew ever saw, and how deeply our bonds would be, and how great it would be to have enjoyed the time at sea together. In my mind's eye I saw the ship sailing romantically over the twenty foot tides, our cabin lit with a dimmed lanterns, and stories being created with every wave that crashed through the deck floor. At the end of the summer, I would collect my wages and return to Tennessee a rich humbled man. Surely, I tell you the illusion of this dream would soon fade, the very second I exited the Anchorage airport.

Coming off the plane, I was filled with excitement. Alaska was a dream I had for a long time. And now, I was there! I walked through the airport with my pack strapped snuggly to my torso, filled with clothing and survival gear. I had only three-hundred dollars in my pocket, but my first thought was to step outside, take in the site, and breathe in the air. As I made my way through the airport, signs filled the walls, "Welcome to Alaska." Pictures of the Iditarod and of the landscape filled my heart with a feeling of awe. As I stepped out of the airport, I stood looking north at the snow covered peaks. I stood with a feeling of great accomplishment. I stood proud. I stood with many questions in my mind. "What would come of this trip?" I thought, as I gazed across the beauty of God's country. With a deep breath and a sigh of uncertainty, I decided it was too late for any mingling and I needed some sleep. So, I entered back into the airport and slept off the anxiety. Though, I was inspired, I was also exhausted. Just getting there was one heck of a leap.

A few hours later, I could wake and conquer the thoughts that had plagued my mind the previous months before landing in this magnificent place. I really believed at this moment dreams were made to come true. And with that thought, I slept comfortably on the emptied bench nestled in the corner of the desolate airport.

As the morning came, I realized the truth about the land of the midnight sun. The sun really does shine all day, even past midnight. Soon, mid-morning approached, and I perched myself upon the bench. As I looked out the windows of the airport, I said, "It's time." I gathered my things and set out for downtown Anchorage. The way I had pictured Anchorage in my mind and its actual layout were two different things. I could not merely walk from one side of town to the other. And there weren't Eskimos and igloos everywhere either. Also, the city had buildings; even a few hotels like the Hilton that could be consider skyscrapers. Restaurants and hotels lined the streets of downtown. It was quite the metropolis. I guess, maybe, I should have done a little more research, but where's the adventure in that? My first twenty dollars was spent on a three or four day bus pass. And my next point of interest was finding a cheap place to sleep. I knew that if there were hostels around, I may even get a free night stay in exchange for cleaning the rooms and restrooms, and so, that's exactly what I did. I found a hostel and dropped off my belongings and hit the streets running. The next step was finding the fishing docks.

As I went to the bay's edge, I noticed there were no fishing vessels, just a small stream flowing in from the bay and a few restaurants and hotels along the shore. I had envisioned a shore with many fishing vessels and docks scattered about, but that wasn't the case. In fact, I saw no boats and no docks at all. So, just walking down to a pier and finding a ship to work on was not going to happen this day. I didn't know what to do. My imagination led me to believe things were different, when, in fact, I left one city for another. My spirit grew low. But then, a little sign of hope appeared. A posted sign on a telephone pole read, "Job Fair: Fishing Industry Seeking Summer Positions." Listed on the flyer were the names of the various fishing vessels and their captains. All I needed to do now was survive one week and get by with what I had. I just knew if I could talk to someone in the fishing industry, I would land the job I had dreamed of for years. Soon my dreams of commercial fishing would become a reality, or at least that's what I thought.

The next few days I went about the city of Anchorage viewing the sights and talking to whoever struck my fancy. My three hundred dollars was dwindling quickly, and after just three days I was down to nearly a hundred dollars. The job fair was still a few days off, and I begin to think I might become a street dwelling hobo. But! I was in the great state of Alaska. And it was time to make some connections, and I knew just the place: church. I realized that I may need a little help from above and my pride may have to be swallowed, and that I may have to allow myself to depend on God for survival. I was preparing my ego for anything. I felt I might become that weakling who might have to reach his hands out and cry, "Rescue me father! I don't know where I am, and I don't know what I'm going to do." I thought a church service would be a good idea. (Isn't that how many of us think? When in need, go to church. If only we could see that we are always in need of God's hand and the rest of His body.) Nevertheless, we take his helping hand for granted daily. Only if we prayed a little more, our problems may be less of a burden, but I guess that comes with time and faith growing experiences.

Looking through the phone book for different churches, I happened to find one on my bus route near the hostel, or so it appeared. After mapping it and figuring the right bus number, I was off to the house of worship. What happened next, however, changed my entire trip. God again interfered with my plans and placed a path more suited for my life's work in front of me. I didn't see it then, but I can see it clear as glass now. And that's always the case with retrospect. God always orchestrates a better plan than the one thought by man. Some say if you want to make God laugh, tell him your plans, and I am a strong believer that this is the truth. And God has laughed a lot with my life and plans.

A few months before departing Tennessee, I had met a young man from Alaska. His name was Roy. He was a young red-headed boy with a golden bushy beard, kind of a mountain'ish and pale looking fella, and I could tell he hadn't tanned much in life. He mentioned that his family had an apartment in the basement of their house in Anchorage. He told me that his dad rents it out from time to time, and I should consider staying there. I told him that I hoped to be at sea within a matter of a few days but would still like to talk with his dad and possibly store some things there if necessary. After calling Roy's dad, Mark Justus, several times and only getting through once to a young boy, who did not know where I could locate Mark, I chose not to worry about the situation. I figured whatever my destiny held would soon place itself in front of me.

Now in Alaska, I would just go and do what I could to survive, and possibly I could try and reach the Justus clan later. I contacted the homeless shelters and spoke of my situation. I stated that I wanted to work and I was not trying to be a vagrant, but I may need a cot for a night or two. I let them know I was waiting for a job opportunity and that I would volunteer for a cot and a meal. Also, I started hitting up some of the motels in the area, thinking if I could just get some work cleaning rooms, I may be able to use an empty room. Also, on my plan was the possibility of finding some temporary work through the people I would later meet at whatever church I decided to attend. And so, with all this in mind, Wednesday night arrived and I was off to make some new friends.

At first I had pictured a small, quaint church nestled in a snow covered valley filled with evergreens and wildlife spread throughout the church yard, but to my surprise when I showed up at the Church on Debarr Street, it was quite a big structure, completely different than what my mind had pictured an Alaskan church to look like. It was in the city, on a city bus route, and as I walked inside, at least two-hundred and fifty to three-hundred members had assembled. "Ha!" I thought. I figured at most the Anchorage churches would have a maximum of twenty to thirty members, but that wasn't the case. I entered the building and sat right on the front pew, and while the study was taking place, I noticed at the other end of the pew a big, burly, peculiar looking man, with long stringy brownish hair and a large bushy beard. He had a funny mannerism about him. In fact, he was the epitome of what I thought an Alaskan man should look like. The pew between us was empty, and behind us the rest of the pews were packed. After the study ended, I proceeded to introduce myself to the big burly man.

"Hello, I'm Jeremy McGill" While shaking hands, the fella looks at me and says, "Hi Jeremy, I'm Mark Justus." I just looked up toward the heavens and laughed; he looked at me oddly and with a look of odd curiosity, wondering why I would act in such a weird way, as to look up in the air and laugh at his introduction. I said to him, "Man, I've been trying to call you for months. I know your son Roy, and I was interested in the apartment you might have for rent. I just gave up because it seemed impossible to reach you." He stared with even more confusion. I explained the whole story, how I had met his son back at the college, back home in Tennessee, and that I had called his home at least six or seven times and left a message with some young boy. He replied boldly with a little frustration in his voice, "Logan! That knuckle head didn't tell me anything. Neither did Roy. Where are you staying now?" I told him I was fine and that for the next few nights, I had a hostel bed and had contacted the shelters, but he didn't like the idea of my sleeping in a hostel or a shelter. Even though it wasn't a big deal to me, he insisted I come with him and stay at his home. After explaining I didn't have any rent for the apartment and I didn't think I was going to be in the city long, he told me, "Don't worry, brother. We're going to pick up your stuff and you're staying with us." He was pretty matter-of-fact about the whole situation. Now, this was pretty amazing to me. Could this have been part of God's plan?

Consider the chances of my sitting by this guy in such a large congregation. Also, there were several churches to choose from in the phonebook, and I ended up at that particular one, sitting by this certain fella. I guess it is true, God does work in mysterious ways. And so it was, I now had new friends and a place to stay. The Justus house would become my temporary dwelling spot, and Mark's wife Sue said the only rule in her house was that I had to eat dinner with them, and that's not a hard rule for me to follow. Isn't it funny how things seem to come together in what may seem to be the most critical times? And this was just the beginning of a beautiful summer.

For the next week, I hung out with Mark and met the people around the block. Every day I could just stare out at the snow covered mountains, and though the snow was disappearing, it was still a beautiful sight, a sight that could be taken in from my new home at anytime. I saw moose running in the streets, salmon swimming up stream in the downtown area. Alaska was truly an amazing place, and at this point I hadn't even got out of the Anchorage city limits. I could tell this would be an easy place for me to live, an easy place for me to call home, and so far in life, having a place to call home isn't something I'm all that familiar with. But there in the great northern state, at that point in life, I felt right at home. The next day, however, things could change. The job fair was about to take place. And my new home may be a ship crewed by a hand-full of dreamy fisherman, waiting for the great catch and the money that followed. Golly, it would be great.

The next morning came and I was off to the job fair. Interview after interview, the same thing happened, "No experience, no luck, and no job." It was explained that since I didn't know someone and because I had no experience, it would be extremely hard for me to get a job on any of these ships; however, there was room in the cannery, but canning fish all summer just didn't sound very appealing. I thought, "Is this something I really want to spend my summer doing in Alaska? No!" And the pay wasn't even that good. A little disheartened, I just walked away. I knew that it was possible that I may not ever return to this place, and I just couldn't see canning fish all summer as any fun at all. 'Experience,' hmmm... that's what they

I knew that it was possible that I may not ever return to this place, and I just couldn't see canning fish all summer as any fun at all. 'Experience,' hmmm... that's what they kept saying. Well if that's the case, I could definitely get a job in the restaurant industry; because, that's something I had vast experience in. Besides that, I was out of money and basically bumming room and board. Having any job sounded better than chasing ships that most likely would never let me board. So, with disappointment, my dream as a sea fisherman came to an end. I've always been a free spirit, and the good thing about that is that it's easy to say, "Okay what's next?" And, so it was again that my plan and God's plan were not in sync.

Returning back to my new found home, I settled into the Anchorage landscape. I needed a job and needed one fast. My experience in the restaurant business would be a plus in the upcoming tourist season. I knew I could land a job in just about any restaurant. All I needed was just one interview, and my chance came at the Glacier Brewhouse as a dishwasher. It's kind of humbling thinking back on that dream of commercial fishing and then to have a college degree and end up working as a dishwasher. But, a man's gotta do what a man's gotta do, and I was glad to be employed.

After a few days of back breaking work in the restaurant, I began to think maybe canning fish would have been better, but that wasn't the choice I made, and now I was stuck. I rode a bike every day from the house to work, working ten to twelve hours, six to seven days a week. The amount of dishes we had to wash was unbelievable.

My feet stayed drenched the entire time. Added to the agony of manual labor was riding the bike three miles back to the homestead every night. The work quickly wore me out, but I had rent to pay and things I wanted to do and see as a guest of this beautiful state.

I wanted to see the deep wilderness, glaciers and eagles. I wanted to camp in the last frontier and catch some salmon as they made their way back up stream to spawn. I even thought about riding a wild whale if I had the chance. So many things to do, and only three months to get it all done, and the only way I was going to be able to make it happen was to work as much and as hard as possible. I also needed a plane ticket back to Tennessee to finish my schooling. So, I worked hard in that dish room, never turning down a shift or overtime. I even got trench foot from being waterlogged and not having boots to wear to protect my feet; eventually, my toenails began falling off, and my skin was wearing away on both feet. It was miserable at first, but I worked hard and long enough that I nearly paid my rent up for the summer. I became friends with many people in the church, and I kept seeing these advertisements for the Midnight Sun Bible Camp. It looked like a magnificent place to spend the summer, and I really wanted to check it out. There was a volunteer opportunity that came along, and I just happened to be off from the brew house that day, and so with my sore feet and exhausted body, I went out to see this place I kept hearing about.

That day, I helped clear the road back to the camp. Trees throughout the winter had fallen on the path that led to the wilderness camp. Seven miles off the main road and a million miles from civilization it seemed. Eventually, we made it to the camp. Sitting there on the Nancy Lake Park was a crystal clear lake, and beautiful evergreens filled the landscape. The air smelled crisp and clean. To the west were snow topped mountains and to the east rolling green valleys filled with wildlife and wild flowers. Setting my eyes on this place, I knew it was where I belonged. I not only wanted to be there but needed to be there. How could I make it work? How could I experience this place? Could I, a stranger show up and offer a helping hand in exchange for experiencing the Alaskan wilderness? Well, it never hurts to flirt? I was told to speak with a Mr. Dave Wallace. I looked around at the camp and knew that if at all possible, this was where I wanted to spend the next month. July in the Alaskan wilderness would be a perfect summer, and all I needed now was Dave's permission.

I returned to Anchorage the following day. I knew that the Midnight Sun Camp was where I belonged, and so I gave the brew house my two week notice. I had made enough money to pay most of my rent. But finding another job until camp arrived seemed to be a good idea. Another fellow at the church, Matt, said he would hire me on at his drywall company. And to make it even better, he would pay me twice what I was making at the restaurant. Everything was coming together. It would be two weeks before the first week of camp, and I couldn't wait. I finished up my last week as a dishwasher, and went fishing for a few days. The week before camp, Matt and I worked side by side hanging drywall and developing a friendship.

Matt was a neat young man; having lived in Alaska all his life, he had built his first log home at age fifteen and homesteaded. I found this quite impressive. Matt had been a commercial fisherman for nine years and knew everyone out in the Bristol Bay. We formed a good friendship that week I worked for him, and Mr. Wallace granted my wish to be a full-time volunteer out at the camp. My time in Alaska was becoming greater every day. The weekend before I left for camp, I was able to afford a glacier cruise, and wow! God's creation really struck a chord in my heart. The land they call Alaska is truly a remarkable place. I watched the glaciers collapse into the sea, sending swells of water into the frigid waters. I saw seals floating effortlessly across the ice sheets that covered the water's surface and the eagles soaring above; it was as if I went back in time, back to a time and place where man had not yet put his footprint. A great feeling of nostalgia and a greater sense of triumph filled my spirit. I was out there and in it all.

There are several tribes that encamp in the Alaskan wilderness such as the Inuit, Haida, and Eskimos. I wasn't sure how far in either direction they might be settled. All I knew was that God created a great place of beauty and awe. And if this moment in the Alaskan journey was but a sampling-taste of heaven's beauty, then we are really in for a sweet surprise in the afterlife, where we walk on streets of gold. It's overwhelming to imagine. The experience would certainly be pivotal into the way I looked at my life and my purpose. As the glacier cruise came to an end, I exited the ship, took a deep breath, stared at the sea one last time, and headed back to my new Alaskan home and began packing for my three weeks at camp.

Things were soon going to change in my life. The internal war within my spirit was soon to be at its most violent point. My bags were packed, and for the most part I knew I would be a stranger amongst the native camp goers; nevertheless, I was enthralled at the thought of being a part of a community that would take on the Alaskan outdoors. And the communal living aspect of it had a charm of its own.

At first, the man in charge of the camp hesitated in letting me stay out there for an entire three weeks. He said most people couldn't make it three weeks out at the camp. "By the third week, they're tired and irritable, and it's a place were your spiritual level needs to be on high." I explained to the wise man that I was the right man for the job and that this is what I live for. "I can handle three weeks, no problem," I stated very matter-of-factly. And to drive my point home, I gave Mr. Wallace a verbal resume. "Sir, I have gone a month living in the streets hitch-hiking from town to town from Tennessee to California. While traveling in Europe for three months, I lived much like a hobo, sleeping under bushes, on park benches, under bridges, and sometimes just in the streets, and as a child, roughing it. Well, that was just a way of life. To stay at the camp would be a treat, a walk in the park, and I really want the opportunity." With my reputation and pride on the line, I was allowed to be a camp counselor, cook, fishing guide, boat operator, and event organizer. Those three weeks at the Bible camp, I thought, would just be a vacation in the wild, but throughout my time there, God was working on my heart and molding his clay.

The lives that surrounded me had meaning. The camaraderie and fellowship were an experience that left me in deep meditation. I understood that God not only existed but he also had an intense love for man. There in the Alaskan wilderness at the Midnight Sun Bible Camp, I begin praying for the strength to lose myself in God's love, to die to self, and, instead of being a sea fishermen, I wondered what it would be like to become a fisher of men. The Christian love that surrounded me there was just as great as the love I had experienced with the Europe group just three years earlier. I understood that I truly needed to lose my pride and become the bride. The bride of Christ submits himself to a life of spiritual trials and struggles. This life will open so many doors to what the world really needs, forgiveness and love. And by the end of camp, I was ready to give in, but just not in that moment. All along I had faked being a Christian just to be part of the family. I knew truly my soul was not in line with the higher power of the angels. I was stubborn to give in.

I figured, if I waited until I got back to Tennessee, I would give in. I would make the commitment. My heart was ready, but the fear of my own personal truths had always held me back. I wanted to become a Christian through repentance and baptism, but I wanted to wait until it seemed that no-one else knew. My pride said to me, "Everyone seems to think you're a Christian. If they knew the truth, you would be cast out as a liar." I wanted to release the disguise, as a man who claimed Christianity, and become a soul immersed in water, forgiven for my fornications, my adulteress ways, my lies, my cheating, my dishonoring of my parents, my murderous mind, my sins that could fill this page and hundreds more, and now all I had to do was make it back to Tennessee. I felt I could confess to the one person I knew wouldn't judge or frown upon my hidden secrets, Garland. He had been a good friend for a few years now, and if the plane didn't crash, I would discuss with him the commitment to follow Christ.

As the summer ended, I saw a family of people who really loved God, a family who didn't want me to leave their Alaskan home. They had known me just a little while, but they were like family. I had just showed up at the door knocking, and they had let the stranger in. Not only did they let me in, but they also fed and clothed me. This love shattered my heart in many respectful ways. It is a love that had changed me from first sight, a love I am glad to have felt, seen, and experienced.

I finished up my summer working with Matt, the drywall man. Honestly, I think we fished more than we worked, and that was fine by me. It was a great feeling knowing at anytime I could return to far north reaches of America. It was a greater feeling knowing I would be accepted as a friend and a brother; nevertheless, I knew had many things I needed to do, finishing my Masters degree and getting to China. So, with another bon voyage to a people who had shaped my life and my life's journey,

I boarded the plane back to Tennessee.

Calmness came over me, and a sigh of relief filled my spirit. Now, it was time to find Garland and reveal my true identity. I knew he would listen and do so with compassionate ears. That August day was one of great relief. I asked Garland to baptize me, and it, like many ordeals in life, was as humorous as others. At first we tried to do so in my bathtub because I didn't want to wait a minute longer, and with his hand on my head and most of my body in the water he tried mashing my head and face under the water, but I was too big for full immersion. It must have given God a good laugh looking at a 150 pound man trying to drown a 250 pound man in a tub fit only for maybe a 200 pound man. As he kept trying to completely immerse me, it was obvious I was too big for the water. "It won't take man! It won't take! You gotta go all the way under," Garland kept saying. I said, "Push harder man, push harder!" Frustrated with the whole scenario and even thinking it was ridiculous to have to be completely under. I stated to Garland, "Let's just go to the lake then." So, we headed down to the lake. There at the mid-south youth camp that August afternoon in swampy, lukewarm water I was completely buried in water baptism. I was by all means forgiven. Buried and resurrected with and in Christ.

I was released from the guilt of crucifying Christ. I knew my hands where on the hammer that drove the nails through his wrists and feet. I knew I was the one who placed the crown of thorns and smashed them on his head and spat in his face all the while mocking him by saying, "King, king of what?" In reality, he was the only one who ever truly loved me. I was the one who he had called out to the father for, "Father, forgive him. He does not know." And all at once my guilt-driven life became grace-centered. My sins were left at the bottom of that lake I was baptized in. I was now filled with a spirit, a holy spirit. A guardian of souls had indwelled within. My future life new and bright, and guarded, a Christian walk had begun, and now I could honestly say "I am a Christian." The mask I had been wearing was no more.

Looking back, I see the importance of the full immersion. It's a simple task God asks us to do. Consider for a moment what it actually represents. It is a burial. Consider the physical burial most of us will have. Our shells that hold our souls are buried. We don't bury just one part of the body, leaving the other exposed to the earth's surface, yet we completely cover the corpse with dirt, never to be seen again, And so, that one simple request, that one obvious command, "Go out and be baptized for the remission of your sins." This is an act of obedience and an action that should be followed. Let no men tell you any different; yet, let the word of God be your guide. It seems as if the Bible is black and white on many issues, and this one just seems to be obvious. The areas of gray, that's another story, but it is stated that only those who have been born of the water shall enter the kingdom.

Beginning my Christian walk has been something extraordinary. Faith comes as you realize your past life no longer exists in the eyes of God. You are a new person, a dead once, born twice living being. The first life was one filled with death and without hope. Those boundaries I loved to cross now have a conscience standing in the way. The life lived before is completely evaporated like the morning dew on a hot summer day. And, as hard as it is to grasp with feeble human minds, that is what God gives us as a gift: the gift called redemption.

God's love is so unbelievable, all consuming, overwhelming, and atoning. And having the faith to believe it and share the light, that's the trial of the new life. Holding the faith, however, seems at times harder that gaining it. Spiritual growth comes with deep, agonizing pain and with a realization that mercy and patience and reverence for God stand center of the growing pains. Yet, there is no other adventure that can top the one led by Christ. Living as a Christian is a test of self and of self-will and losing it all again and again repeatedly for Him and His will.

Thinking back, I used to want to be the tough guy. I wanted to be the guy with all the toys and scantily clad women on my side. I wanted to be envied by the world, an outlaw like Jesse James. Now, however, I hope to be seen not as a good man, but as a light of Christ, a new and forgiven man, because I, by myself, can do no good. Yet, my boldness stands in God's mercy and love. I went to Alaska to go fishing; I came back to Tennessee remembering what Jesus had said to me long ago on the shores of Galilee, "Come and I will make you a fisher of man's souls." And I'm here to say, there's no greater calling and I'm thankful for all those who helped me get here simply by loving me with the love of Christ. Now, with all this said, let's go to China! I guarantee the story will deepen your faith as I learned what it meant to be a fisher of men.

## *The Road to China: Romantic Chains*

(IF YOU DON'T HAVE A SENSE OF HUMOR, SKIP THIS CHAPTER)

The story of Bob was my first inspiration, but now as a new Christian I had to ask myself, "What next?" I had a great interest in traveling, and the thought of completely indulging myself in another culture seemed fascinating. And who better to love on than a people who are known to be mostly atheistic? This was a good incentive, and in China, I felt I could make a difference. I figured that after all God had done for me, I could at the least give a year to carry out the great commission. My calling for a while had been China. Some may say it was already written in the book of destiny. I suppose that may just be; but creating our own destinies through the many paths placed before us just seems more sensible. It's good not knowing the future, but it's great to have a path less traveled to embark on. Nevertheless, I wasn't in China yet. I still had some T's to cross and I's to dot, and some romantic issues to work out.

Life sure changes fast on spiritual roads. One second you think you've got it all figured out. You think you have boxed God in with manipulation and the excuse that "I AM ONLY HUMAN!" And then, in between these thoughts, he does what he does best and fathers you into a deeper love for himself. I thought the last year at the university all my prayers would be answered overnight. My main prayer was to have a woman's love enter my life and that she would become my wife and mother to my children. I even fell for a lady. Everything was smooth going. I thought she might be the one, but again another heart-break. I hesitated writing about this love affair, but writing is how I vent, and maybe someone else will be able to relate, or maybe you may find yourself needing a softer heart.

I fell in love with a Pharisee's daughter, and it left me on the brink of leaving the church. There is law, and Jesus says, "Those who love me will do as I command." Yet, at the same time, the Pharisee leaders who wanted to crucify Christ the most were by all means, men of faith and law. Yet, their legalistic views on their fellow man, and their hardened hearts blinded them on what really mattered the most, and that was compassion for the sinner and for all mankind. We are to love our brother with unconditional love, and though we all fail at this, one would think an elder would have such a love as this.

I was a new Christian and what I experienced in dating this lady will forever affect me. Yet, my loyalty is to God, and I will love all people regardless of how hard their hearts may be and regardless if they have done me wrong or anyone else. Everyone needs compassion. The situation left me with three basic rules, and I like to share these rules with my fellow hell-raisers turned Christian. Three rules to follow for those of us who may not have the greatest reputations:

Rule # 3: If by chance you have a rocky past and maybe you have found yourself in the crossbar hotel a time or two, don't date the policeman's daughter. Just save yourself the trouble. You have no chance. There's no such thing as rehabilitated man.

Rule # 2: If by chance you are not the essence of a scriptured, boxed in, traditional, stereo-typed conservative, robotic, Christian, do not date the elder's daughter. It's probably not going to work out; Jesus came a long time ago, and that may be the only one good enough for her.

Rule # 1: The most important rule, if by chance you have had a promiscuous, self-indulging, self-centered life with all the red flags a man can have, RUN! Run from the daughter of the man who is both a cop and an elder. It's all heartache. Take my word for it; don't worry about what the hoipoli thinks. Know that Jesus forgives, and since you're not Jesus, you most likely don't have a snowballs chance in hell at dating the daughter of a man whose reputation may be tainted by your entering his family. Though I would have loved that lady with all my heart, I understood that I was never good enough for her family, but as God stands before me, I can accept the consequences of my past. He's forgiven me, and I forgive them that prematurely judged me. Hopefully, one day God will send me that angel I continually pray for. And in the words of Forest Gump, "That's all I got to say about that." Moving right along, a chain was broken, and China was still a go.

January 2007 would be my last semester at the university. I had started there nearly seven years ago. My plan upon first entering the university was to get in and out as quickly as possible. Make no friends, just keep my head down, don't get noticed, do my work and make C's to just get by. I figured within three and half years I would receive a degree and a teaching license and be done with that rigid Christian school. I felt like an outsider when I first enrolled. I felt like all the inner-circles were saying, "What's that wretch doing here?" Now, as I have stated before, my plans and God's plans seem to be running in opposite directions, however, every now and again our paths somehow amazingly find a meeting place, a crossing so to speak and fitting perfectly into place.

One afternoon, I found myself talking to the president of the university, explaining my story and my plans upon first arriving. I stated to President Sewell, "Sir, I planned for three and half years, but I've been here seven. I planned one degree; now, I have two, one which is a Masters. I was the kid who was given a diploma to leave high school at age twenty. Now, I'm nearly a strait A graduate student, who hates a B. Sir, I planned on making no friends; now I have more friends than I can shake a stick at. Sir, I didn't want any part of that Christian love, but now I am leaving a missionary for China, and I'm hoping to share God's love with the entire world. And Sir, if that's not God, I don't know what God is." I felt the president of the school needed to know that Freed-Hardeman had done more than just educate me. In fact, FHU had stuck to its motto and given me a future beyond belief.

Through the Christian education I had received, God was able to find me. And as wretched as I am, I was still a useable vessel to God, for God. I was ecstatic about my last semester in the graduate program. Thoughts of China and the adventure filled my mind. Everything was in place for me to leave out in the coming fall. Nevertheless, China wasn't my only thought. Thoughts of romance and love for a woman and the desire for children plagued my mind as well. Would either ever come?

In the midst of all my thoughts and anxieties, on a Tuesday night class, she entered my life again, my little Russian princess, Ally. After the failed relationship with the elder/cop's daughter, she couldn't have come at a greater time and at the same exact moment, possibly the worse moment. I had plans for China, and she, well, I believe her dream was here in America. Our first date was Valentines night. And sure enough, before all was said and done, I found myself falling quickly again. What can I say? I'm a romantic and I know it, it's just part of my make-up. I'm so weak when it comes to women, much like Sampson, I suppose.

Ally and I began forming a great bond. Our dating nights increased, and we spent a lot of time together that spring semester. Ally became my new best friend; Ally, however, was also a very challenging girlfriend. She was very structured and sophisticated, and me... well, I'm a little free spirited and completely impulsive. Nonetheless, we took trips to Kentucky, Chattanooga, and just anywhere that held neat, unique beauty, like the highland rim caverns and waterfalls of East Tennessee. I even taught the young city girl how to fish, and, believe it or not, she was a natural. We were having a great time and a great spring, but summer was nearing, and I would soon sail off into the eastern sunset for my adventures in Asia. I thought Ally may just become a mere special memory. In fact, I told her I was just there for a moment, but then a twist of fate.

My plans for graduating in May and heading back to Alaska were interrupted by a clerical era in the university's data base. Ends up, I needed to take one more class in the summer in order to fulfill my financial aid requirements. My plans for Alaska were now stalemated. I had planned to fly from Alaska to China where I had been hired as a university English professor. I would have left early in the summer for Alaska, flown back to Alabama for a training series, and by August, I would be leaving for Asia. No ties, no good-byes, no chains, no problems, that's the way I saw it. But, as fate had it, I ended having to spend my summer in the small town of Henderson. However, I decided to make the most of my summer. I spent the summer preparing for China, reading different books and watching videos. I spent my time thinking of the limitless possibilities of what could happen after arriving in the Far East. But, I also found myself in turmoil, because, I was enchanted by Ally's gentleness and beauty. Had I fallen for my complete opposite? Many people say that opposites attract, and if there were ever two people from two different worlds, it was definitely Ally and I.

Ally was reared in a very structured home, where

seemingly everything was in order, sophisticated, and disciplined. I, on the other hand, was reared by hillbilly-hippies where everything was free and chaotic and not so civilized, kind of "redneckish" one might say. She was the least likely person to walk beside me, and man did we have our fights, both being strong-minded, stubborn, set in our ways, not ever wanting to give in because of our pride. However, when things were great, they were really great. I always loved hearing her say my name. Sometimes, I would do something so unsophisticated and outrageous that she would look at me, and with a deep, subtle, exaggerated, disappointed Russian accented voice say, "Jerremeee." Her face would be red from embarrassment and her eyes gleaming with fury at me. Sometimes she would just walk away from me as if she didn't know me. This happened almost everywhere we went.

On one trip to D.C., we were on the subway. I decided to pole dance for the passengers on the crowded subway. These kind of things made her regret that she even liked me in the slightest manner, but that's my personality, and I love entertaining and making people laugh. And what could be funnier than a two-hundred and fifty pound man with a straw hat, pole dancing on D.C. subway car? So many things I did embarrassed Ally. Truly, if there was such a thing as a match made in heaven, we must have completed the wrong survey. Nevertheless, I would soon depart, and what of it? I was committed to teaching in China, I wanted to explore the world, live life to its fullest, and quite possibly have a Bob story of my own. And, to have this experience, I would have to leave all behind, even the chance of love and romance.

At first, when I found out I was not going to get to head back to Alaska, I was a little disheartened, but having Ally around made everything alright. Soon the summer would end and with a kiss and a tear, I told Ally goodbye and headed for the Ancient East. I thought I would be able to forget Ally once overseas, but it was too late the love bug had gotten me. Yet, nothing could hold me down. I had a mission, and I was going to complete it. I figured whatever destiny held would take place, and if she were to be my lady, she would wait, and I would love her from a distance. Once again, my heart's desire for love and adventure were at odds. I chose to travel, all the while shackled by romantic chains. Nevertheless, the road to China was paved, and off I sailed.

## *Welcome to China:*
## *Ni' Hao*

August 2007: As I stepped off the plane into the China landscape, I was overwhelmed with excitement. I was in a city called Wuhan. Wuhan is set in the Hubei province. The atmosphere had a great awkwardness about it, and all sorts of questions filled my mind. I had two fellow Americans with me who would be teaching at the same school. Their names were Adam and Lucy. Once through the airport, we found a man holding a sign which listed our three names, "Welcome Adam, Lucy, and Jeremy." The dream of visiting the Ancient East was now a reality. The reality of my naiveté set in. For a few years now, China was only a thought, and suddenly it became a reality. I was really there and there to stay for a while. It was no vacation, though it may have seemed like one. In fact, it was my job, my duty, and I had no idea what to really expect.

The streets were not as clean as those back home. The city had eight million registered citizens. The yellow dividing lines on the road seemed to have no meaning and everyone drove crazily. I saw buses drive upon curbs to go around other vehicles. And speed limits? There was no such thing. The Chinese way of driving was to race in front of the next guy. If your front bumper was in front of the other guys, you had the right-of-way. Sounds of horns filled the streets. The loudness of the city and all the

Chinese language being spoken filled my ears with mass confusion. Food vendors cooking odd-looking delicates strolled about the sidewalks. Chicken feet, chicken heads, squid, corn on the cob, duck, duck intestines, different types of vegetables, tofu, and other things I'm not so sure I really wanted to know about were being grilled on the spot. The vendors had rolling grills that lined each and every sidewalk. The atmosphere was one of unfamiliarity and one of amazement. Looking around at the city streets, I saw that more taxis, mopeds, and buses filled the roadways than did personal automobiles. And there were people everywhere. It was as if I stepped off a jet plane onto another planet full of thin, little dark-haired people. I did love this feeling and knowing I was the alien made it all the more intriguing. Many questions ran through my mind.

Would I be accepted? Had I made the right choice? My heart had guided me here, but was it really the right decision? China was my new home, and though everything was new, a subtle peace came over me, and I was ready to start this journey. Call it what you will, but I think I'm part lizard, able to adapt to most any situation and place. It's a gift I'm glad God placed within me. Worrying has never been part of my mode of operation. And as I looked at the city around me, I knew in an instant, without a doubt, I was exactly where I belonged, and I was ready to take on the challenges.

The first few days Adam, Lucy, and I spent our time finding food markets and getting acquainted with our new campus and with each other. The Chinese people were wonderful at making us feel at home. They were very respectful and courteous to our situation. It seemed everywhere we went people were watching our every move. We stood out like that huge juicy white pimple in the center of your forehead. But instead of being filled with disgusting puss, we were ready to burst with love and excitement on our new friends. The Chinese called me strong man when I first arrived; so, I decided I would walk around with my gut sucked in and walk like Arnold Swartzneiger. I felt huge and muscular, until eventually my bubble was popped. Lucy explained that 'strong man' meant 'fat man,' and then my posture went back to normal. I slouched. Oh well, it was a good feeling while it lasted. So, if the Chinese wanted to call me strong, I would say, "Yes, strong man eats many Chinese people." And with quotes like this, it didn't take long before I noticed I was speaking Chenglish. Chenglish is when an English speaking person talks like a Chinese person with poor English skills or vice versa. And, honestly, it comes naturally, I can hear myself using the Chenglish language even today, saying things like "You go that way. I show you." Short, small, fragmented sentences filled most of my conversations, and I tried to do it with a Chinese accent. It's a hard habit to break because you want everyone to understand what you're talking about. And because I understood very little, my Chinese name became 'Ting bu Dong," which means 'I don't understand.' Very fitting, wouldn't you say?

Within a few days, we were settled in and China became home, and all was comfortable. I was loving my life, my students, my peers, and my faculty. The food was amazing, and life was easy going. I felt that, I was on top of the world. As a child from the other side of the tracks, I never imagined having such a prestigious title as 'professor.' Much less, I never expected to be a teacher at a Chinese university, but it was the real deal, and I loved it. The Chinese truly catered to us. My sixteen-hour work week enabled me to form many relationships. Some days I would just ride the bus to get lost and walk the streets. I would go into any random store and talk to anyone I could, even if they didn't speak English. And when they didn't speak English, I would use the whole 'maybe if I yell they will understand.' Of course, that never helped, but it sure was fun to do. Within a matter of weeks, I had a great number of Chinese friends, and every Sunday I would have a 'party' and they would come visit. We would sing songs, lift up one another, and discuss what our hearts desires' were, and if the mood provoked we would talk about 'The God' and the Bible. We did so in a secret manner for fear of outside interference, and fear is not one thing I comprehend very well.

To understand the fear the Chinese live with, you must understand that the country is made up of mostly atheistic people. The studies show that 95% of the population has no belief in God. Three percent are Buddhist, and the other remaining two percent happen to be Christians. And the Christians are the ones who are most persecuted. The government fears religion because they see it as a threat to governing with a strong fist. If, by chance, people believed in something besides what the government offered, they may not be easily controlled.

Chinese are taught from a young age that if you believe in a God, you are ignorant; rather, they say you should believe in yourself, your government, and occasionally some reveal their ancestors as Gods. The Chinese Communist Party (CCP) controls everything. Every entity of the infrastructure of China is governed under communist regulations. Even on religion the government has its nose watching for any sign of rebellion against Maoist loyalists. There is actually a thing called the three-self church. And, basically, it is just a way to appease the people who want to call themselves Christians, and I believe the whole purpose of this government church is to keep an eye on foreigners who want to try and change the system of government. Just to give you an idea of what the governed 'international' church does, I must explain their worship services. They do not allow the Chinese citizens to worship with the foreigners; therefore, it is a regulated church run by the communist government. The same government that teaches its people that God is only for fools. As an American, I just can't help to see it as anything but a wall of oppression. It is why the first colonists came to America, to escape religious tyranny.

Take, for example, the idea that I was married to a Chinese woman, and we decided to go to the international church; we would not be allowed to worship together. She would be separated from me and taught one thing, while I would be separated by a wall from her, being taught another thing, and I ask you now, would you call this true Christianity? This is exactly why the first European-Americans left the British rule, to be free from Pharisaical rule. Even though this international church existed, it was not even heard of in most other cities in China. Chinese have little tolerance for Christian churches. So, Americans and other people of democracies, count your religious freedoms as a great blessing. You have more than you realize.

China was an awesome experience. My first week teaching, I was shocked by the invitations to so many places by many of my students. I told them I hoped to one day visit each place, but honestly, I didn't feel we had enough time. The students all got to choose their own English names. I found this quite humorous. Some chose names like Bob, Will, Mason, Julie, Amy, and Charlotte, while others were more creative choosing names like, Pink, Sunshine, Wing, Garlic, and Hyser. I even had a young man that wanted to be called Darling. And, so it was, I had my students, and they had their new American teacher.

My class was filled with personalities and the brightest of China's population. They were all respectful and courteous, always early to class, and always on task. Those who make it to the college level had to pass an insurmountable amount of testing. It's an honor to make the university level; many by the age of fourteen know they're not cut out for the college path, and their middle schools tell them so. Those who are dropped from the education system are forced into a life of labor. For the most part, many end up learning a trade like farming, construction, or retail. It is nothing like the U.S. education system. Regardless of intelligence in America, we have No Child Left Behind. Everyone has a chance to graduate from high school, again another blessing from being a citizen in the U.S.A.

In the U.S. we have so many opportunities. Take me, for instance; I graduated at the bottom of my high school class and was basically given a diploma to leave high school at age twenty. Now, I have a Masters degree and plan to pursue a PhD. The U.S.A. is not called the land of opportunity for nothing; I heard it once said, "Here in the United States we can just pick a job and do it." I think, for the most part, this statement is true. Not all succeed, but those who are willing to work their tales off have a great chance of achieving their dreams. In America we are blessed with many unseen riches. Everyone has an equal chance. Nevertheless, let's dive back into China. Maybe some other day, in some other book, we can discuss our freedoms and that which may be lost if we aren't careful in protecting our precious Constitution.

Traveling in such an ancient place as China really does impress upon the mind of human triumph. Humanity has come so far, yet, in this world of technology, there are so many still living as if the twentieth century never existed. In China, I saw peasants in the fields as I traveled the countryside by train. I saw people carrying baskets of fruit with bamboo poles topped and balanced on their shoulders. To cut the grass, I saw a dozen men on their hands and knees with sickles, laboring manicure the landscape. Many lived in shacks along lakes that contained the fish they would sell in the markets. The street vendors offered great meals for less than one U.S. dollar. The smells of spices and fried foods filled every street. There are also beggars with obvious disabilities, and on many streets dimly lit shop corners with pink lights, showcased young girls no older than fifteen prostituting themselves. Some of these girls were sent by their families for finances. Just taking a stroll down the street, I would see many sad, tired lives. I would guess that 90 percent of the Chinese population had worked hard all their lives and had very little to show for their labor. Maybe one child in a million made it to college, but then his or her responsibility was to care for his or her family. Life in China, at a glance, seems ancient and rigid, but despite these truths, the people are very warm, loving, and colorful.

One thing that surprised me was that some marriages are arranged through an agreement of the families due to survival needs. Though I saw many hard, rough lives, I also saw many shining faces. Many times I was asked by students, co-workers, and strangers, "Why you so happy all dee time?" My response may have varied, but mostly it would have been something like this: "Life's too short to be sad, and one day I'll have heaven. I know this because Jesus loves me." Most of the time they smiled at the thought, or maybe they just smiled because I gave them an answer of hope. We never know what another thinks, but we can always express our love. Besides, why wouldn't I be happy? I was living out my dream. I was a traveling teacher exploring the world and filling my life with other cultures. I loved my job.

Experiencing a culture so deep and rich with history was such a delight. We are all a sum total of our experiences, and so this China experience was being added to my total being. As a total sum of myself, I had experienced many things in life. At that present moment, I was a traveling professor. I was able to view many wonders of the world like the Terracotta Warriors in X'ian and the Great Wall of China. I had already traveled many places in the U.S. and in Europe, but of all my travels, this China trip was the most fascinating, and the people welcomed me with warm, open arms. The relationships I built there will be long lasting, and most likely lifelong.

One of my favorite students, Michael took me to X'ian and we climbed the ancient city walls. Then, with a group of his peers, we embarked on a journey climbing one of the five sacred mountains of China, Mt. Huashan. The neatest part of that climb was that we did so at night. We did the night trek to watch the sunrise the next morning. Another amusing thing was that we weren't alone in our climb, hundreds, possibly thousands, of other climbers were doing the same thing that evening. It was like a mass pilgrimage in which everyone was all on the same team, with the same destination in mind. Everyone cheered the next climber on. "You can make it!" Thinking back on that moment today, I have an overwhelming feeling of awe and oneness with the Chinese.

Being a part of that climb on that festive evening will always be a treasure in my heart. It was a time of great reflection, and there amongst a thousand or so Chinese people on top of a very steep mountain, watching the sunrise to the east gave me an intense feeling of purpose. We had climbed all night long, and our bodies were worn out. Yet, the light of the sunrise gave us hope and energy.

For about thirty minutes we all stood as one, watching a new day birth into existence. Experiences like this are what I want my sum total to be. Camping outside the Great Wall along the Mongolian border on top of a freezing mountain with Adam Davis, in the snow, that's what I want my sum total to have within it. Everyone measures success in different ways. I hope that whatever success God allots me, I give him all the glory. I hope I never label my success by the things I have, but rather by the love I shared. I have issues with American materialism. More so, people measure success by the cars they drive, by the mansions they live in, or by the number of toys they have. All these material things will certainly rust away. No-one remembers what possessions a person has; rather, when buried, people remember how they lived their lives. Did they love others, or did they love themselves more? At our deaths our truths are met, and soon enough my death and my truths are going to meet me In a way I will never forget.

I pray to God to give me a cup over flowing with real life experiences, experiences that mirror Him who created me, and magnify my soul. This is a battle I fight daily. I too want the nice things here on earth, and I think there is nothing wrong with having nice things, but seeing a modest China man living happily with very little makes me sometimes feel selfish and full of greed. I hope one day I can provide a family with a nice home and a few nice luxuries. I hope, however, I never place these things above the greatest thing a man can give his family, and that's the knowledge of God's unbelievable love. Thinking deeply on this, I wonder what good does it do to have all the toys in the world, to be the envy of men who base there lives on objects of decay? If I had the whole world as my possession, and I didn't enter heaven, my life served only myself and my own desires. And in that way, a man who has it all but doesn't have God is truly the most poverished man of all.

Can you imagine lying on your deathbed? Can you imagine thinking, "I had it all, a three story house, a hot rod, a motorcycle that shined in the sun, a yacht, a house on the beach and another home in the mountains. I lived like a king and all men wanted to be like me." Then, as your eyes quivered shut and you took your last dying breath, Jesus appeared before you. By his side was that homeless, beggar you left penniless as you went and filled your stomach at an overpriced restaurant. Then Christ looked at you in your fading moments and says, "You had the good life, but you chose not to include me. I had said long ago the humble and poor shall inherit the kingdom. I wish I knew who you were but I never caught your name." And just like that, life meets eternity. The funny thing is, it can happen at any second, and later you will find it almost happened to me. However, before we get to that point, I want to introduce you to Kenji. Kenji is one of my best friends, and he, to me, is the greatest part of this entire story. Kenji is and will always be, a true best friend.

## Welcome to China: Kenji

All was well there in China. I had plenty of friends and was connected to a few Christians. My Sundays were spent riding my bike across the city looking for a family to be with on Sundays. I couldn't believe it. Just a few years back, Sunday mornings used to be filled with drunken hangovers and blackouts. But due to my new found faith, a Sunday without worship, without thanking God for giving me hope seemed dull and empty. I had met some Chinese Christian families through various contacts, but nothing felt right. I wanted a deep connected family, and God knew my prayers were to have such a fellowship. It was something my spirit longed for. Even my American co-workers had found their Christian connections, but I kind of felt like I was standing alone on Sundays. Then, a call from a man named Tyler came.

"Hey man, my name is Tyler. Someone gave me your name, and I was wondering if you had a place for me and my family to meet on Sundays. I want to meet you first, but we really need a safe place to meet." My immediate reply, "Absolutely brother, you can have a key to my house. My home is your home." Later that week Tyler and I met, along with him was a few of the Chinese Christians. Not all of them spoke English fluently or clearly, and some hardly spoke any English. Nonetheless, we knew enough to communicate the important things that would happen between us in the following weeks to come. We all warmed up to each other pretty quickly, and Sunday's meeting time was set. My heart's prayer was answered. I now had a Chinese, Christian family of my own.

Sunday rolled around and I became acquainted with them, not only as friends but as brothers who needed me just as much as I needed them. Leslie, Fish, Wing, Sammy, Ting Ting, Tyler, and the others piled into the living space of my dwelling. In the group that entered, one man in particular stood out more than the others to me. Maybe it was his demeanor, his quirkiness, or maybe it was his genuine interest in my life; nevertheless, I found this young China man warm hearted and sincere. His name was Kenji. He was a person I could see myself growing close to very easily. He was funny, honest, and a little goofy. We definitely had matching personalities, and so after our first Sunday meeting, Kenji sat around an extra hour or so just talking with me. I can't remember what we talked about, but I do remember laughing a lot. Eventually, they had all left, but I had a humble peacefulness set in my heart, and I felt certain that God had placed these wonderful people in my life for a reason he only knew. After our first meeting, it seemed that the next Sunday couldn't come soon enough.

By this point in the trip, I could tell teaching was a natural ability for me. My students often said, "Mr. Jeremy, you so funny, but so strict. It seems a little strange to us." I explained, "Learning can be fun, but if I give you any slack, you will never try and reach a higher level, and my job as a teacher is to elevate your English to the highest level possible." The students were used to easy going foreign teachers, but I was serious and they respected that, and I sure loved my students. I can sit here and think back and see all of them now. I guess I'm becoming an old softy because I cry at the thought of my first students. Many of them never heard the words "I Love You," and here I was, a stranger, repeating these words to them each and every day possible. They were a delight and another part of my total sum. I probably learned more from them than they did from me. But that's the way it usually goes when one teaches with love in his or her heart. The weeks sometimes went slowly by, but that first week after my first meeting with my Chinese family couldn't go by fast enough. I was ready for Sunday to arrive. I missed my new found family, and I wanted to hug them all. Soon Sunday came, and it was as if we had all known each other our entire lives. Everything flowed naturally, and when the evening meeting was over, and they began to exit back to their weekly lives, an interesting thing happened. Kenji, with his cute China accent, said, "I think, I live with you tonight?" I understood he wished to spend the night with me, and I guessed he wanted to observe my way of life. I told Kenji it would be a delight to have company for the evening. The funny thing is, Kenji never left, and I was glad.

During the days we worked. I worked with the university, and Kenji worked with his corporation. Every night we would meet up, have dinner together, and poke fun of each other. I loved making fun of Kenji's Chenglish. He also thought my Chinese was hideous and hilarious. A southern man speaking Chinese has to be completely off, "Don't yall readers agree?" Kenji and I were like two peas in a pod. I loved making Kenji upset with my American antics, and I played the foreign ticket to its extreme. There's nothing funnier than seeing a Chinese man upset. Often I would say with my Chenglish voice, "Kenji, you Chinese, you know nothing. Americans know everything and that's the way it is." He would in return say, "Ahhh, you know nothing, Chinese know Eevrrrrything." We had a genuine brotherly relationship.

I also knew Kenji followed every law of the land. He used every cross walk and yielded at every yellow sign whereas the rest of the population just crossed the streets any and everywhere. To most people, those lights seemed to have no meaning. One day Kenji and I were walking to the market, and I dashed across the busy road through all the traffic. I figured he was right behind me, but by the time I had crossed the street and looked back, I saw him still standing there. He had a disappointing look on his face. I knew what I had done scared him and he was mad about it. He briskly walked down to the cross walk, never taking his eyes off me, staring with fury in his mind. His expression was that of an angry Chinese man, and I was laughing hysterically because I knew he was fixing to let me have it. By the time he made it down the sidewalk to where I was waiting for him, he begin saying loudly, "YOU! You shouldn't do that! You are a Christian! You suppose to follow all laws!" I laughed even louder. He remarked, "Ahh. American, soooo stupid sometimes. Never listen to anything." I really miss those days of harassing Kenji, but I can honestly say our brotherly love for each other was as strong as any relationship I had ever had. Kenji would do anything for me, and I would do anything for him.

I remember one time we went fishing, and we were catching these little bitty fish. I always poked fun of the Chinese to get a rise out of Kenji, and on this particular day I was going to mess with Kenji about the size fish we were catching "Kenji, in America we only catch the big fish. These Chinese fish are small fries like you." He, without hesitation, sat his pole down and disappeared for a moment. I wondered what in the world he was up to. I was sure a retaliation of some sort was about to happen. Then, he came back and said, "Okay, you want big fish, we go and catch big fish."

I was just joking around with Kenji, but somehow he had arranged a car to come pick us up and take us to a lake that had big fish. I was amazed at his gesture. He truly wanted me to be happy in every way possible. Once we arrived at the lake, I saw that it was full of four to six feet long carp, and the poles we used were probably fifteen feet long, with no reels. They were huge bamboo poles, made telescopically with a line tied to the end. The idea behind the long poles was once you hooked the fish, you had to retract the extended rod back into itself, then grab the line and pull the fish in. It seemed a difficult way to fish, but that's the fun of being in another culture, and to me it made it more fun. So, there we were by the waters edge. I took my huge bamboo pole and threw my line out into the small pond-like lake. Kenji just stepped back and watched. Then he said, "You know, when you catch the big fish, you have to pay for it?" I looked at Kenji like he was crazy. I explained, "Kenji, I ain't paying for this fish, I just want to catch one. I will throw it back in and let it live another day." "Oh no!" he replied, "The rule says you catch, you must pay." Again, I said, "Kenji, I'm not paying for a carp. In America we throw these fish back." He again, with disgust in my rebellion says, "Ahhh, American never, never do anything right!" And about that time, Wham! A giant carp grabbed my hook. The fight was on and it was quite exciting seeing the monstrous fish splashing about the top of the waters surface. All eyes were on me as I screamed "Wooo-hooo! Kenji, we gotta big'n."

The man who managed the lake came running with a net in hand. Then, suddenly he tried to grab the fishing pole out of my hand. So now, not only was I struggling with this fish but also the Chinese man who was trying to wrestle the pole out of my hand. Amidst all the chaos, I begin yelling at Kenji, "Tell this man to let go of my rod! Tell him I'm a professional!" The two began talking loudly to each other in Chinese. I couldn't understand anything they were saying, but eventually the man let go of the bamboo fishing pole, and I landed a five foot carp into the net. Once the chaos stopped and the fish was calm, I looked at Kenji with a big mischievous smile. He knew I was fixing to release the fish back in the water. He knew I did not want to pay for it, and so I looked at the man who had tried to help me get the fish in, and I said loudly, "You know what we do with these fish in America?" He looked at me confused, and Kenji just looked down at the ground shaking his head in disappointment. I said to the man, "This is what I do with these fish!" I took and quickly put the fish back into the water. "Ahhhh!, Ching! Ting Pang! Ding ping dong! Ching!

Chang! Watta watta bing Bang!" I had no idea what the man was saying. I just knew he wasn't very happy. So, I did the only thing I knew to do and just started yelling one of the only phrases I knew, "Ting Bu Dong! Ting Bu Dong! Ting Bu Dong!" (Remember this is also my name, which means, I don't understand). Then, with all the yelling going on, I told Kenji to tell him the fish wasn't big enough. This only added to the stir of emotions that was going on., for the fish was plenty big enough. I just loved the humor of the situation.

Kenji then begin to translate for the both of us, the manager of the lake and myself. Before the whole event was over, an agreement was made. If I would come back and teach the man's daughter English, I could fish for free at any time. That was a beautiful day for me, full of humor and excitement. As we left, Kenji looked over at me with a slight grin, "You, you always cause the problem." I must admit, I am a little mischievous; it's my nature. I told the man that after the winter break, I would come back and gladly teach his daughter English. I gave him a hug, and he accepted my embrace. I told him I would even pay for the next fish I caught. Kenji translated all of this, of course.

Now, winter was approaching and the Christmas spirit was in the air. I knew most Chinese had very little knowledge of what Christmas truly was about. I did see some pictures of Santa Claus in shop windows, and some even had fake trees decorated with lights. Seeing this made me think deeply about the impact Christmas has had on the world. It seems the Chinese view this season merely no more than a festive time to eat, drink, and be merry, a time where presents are exchanged and parties are held. Agreeably, in a sad way I guess that's probably a good view, and I would guess the rest of the world probably holds true to this perception, in particular Americans and the way we celebrate the season. In the U.S., all know the story of Jesus, and this may be the one time of year some step into a church setting, but for me, the celebration of my savior's life should be a daily thing. I'm glad somewhere in Catholic history a person proposed the idea of a 'Christ Mass,' but throughout the years it has become a materialistic celebration, rather than a celebration of spiritual hope. When I see this Western sphere of influence in the Chinese culture, it saddens me to know that most have no idea of why a nation under God truly celebrates Christmas.

A few years ago, I gave my last Christmas gifts to my family. I got them all Bibles with their names engraved on them. I wrote each of them a letter explaining that I was going to celebrate Christmas without gift-giving from this day forward, and I would appreciate it if they did not offer me any gifts. I stated in my letters to each of them that if the last Christmas gift I gave them was the story of Christ, the story which can save their souls, then, I had given them a door to the greatest gift they could ever receive. My hope in such a bold rejection of the traditional Christmas celebration was not that of a humbug. I really wanted my family to open God's word and realize that something huge had to have happened over 2000 years ago, something so amazing that the entire world banks on a calendar stemmed from this historical event. Something that stopped and started time all at once, and the only answer is Jesus Christ, the Messiah.

'Reader,' have you ever really stepped back and thought about your death? Death is part of life. Some people, like presidents and world leaders and heroes of different types will be honored annually. However, only one time in history has a person been born that not only stopped time, but also started time with his life and death (Hint B.C.E and A.D). I don't care how great a person you may think you are, your death will not have a calendar based on it; maybe your relatives and a few close friends will remember your birth. Maybe even a tattoo of a loved one is now engraved on your body somewhere. But Christ's life turned the world upside down and now everyone in the world banks on the Christian calendar. That to me is overwhelming evidence, and I need no other proof than that to realize a Christ was born, and today we do live in a time called 'Anno Domini' (AD) which is Latin, meaning in the year of our Lord. No other religion has done this, not Budha, not Mohammed, and not the god's of mythology. The proof is overwhelmingly obvious. I hope you see that.

It is my hope in the end that not only my family, but everyone who may read this book, opens that trusting word of God and allows His love to lead them into a place we cannot even imagine, that place we like to call heaven. It is there, and it is achievable. You just gotta get the faith. Let no one tell you different, let no denomination rule your life. Your soul is your responsibility, so give it to God, and he will do the rest. And if you don't believe me now, wait until we get the climax of this story, where I was found alone on a jungle path broken and bleeding with my intestines hanging out. The chance for survival was zero. I cried out to the Lord for mercy, and he reached his mighty hand out and showed me that miracles really do happen. I state boldly here, the Juice I offer in this book will leave you thirsty and wanting more. This 'thing' I call 'Elephant Juice' is real. And it's a story I must share with the world, but for now let us continue on with a little more about Kenji. By now I'm sure most of you would love to meet Kenji, and hopefully, one day he will visit America, and I will show him true American culture.

With Christmas in the air, I was planning a huge party in my new Chinese apartment. All people were invited and it was going to be the smash hit of the year. I bought tons of food, chopped lamb, veggies of every kind, fruit, pies, cookies, skinned dogs and cats, and any creature that may walk…just kidding PETA people. Seriously, I decorated my apartment with thousands of lights, and I even went and cut down a live Christmas tree. Later I found out it wasn't quite legal to cut down trees in China, but I needed one, and it was too late, the tree was up and fully decorated. Besides, what's Christmas without a tree?

I spotted the special little evergreen on a bus ride through town. It was a perfect five foot green cedar. When I saw it, I immediately got off the bus and walked over to it. Yep, all the branches were in perfect alignment. "This is the one," I said to myself. It would be the best tree China ever saw. From there, I went down the street and bought a saw. Then, I proceeded back to the tree. Sure, I had to jump a wall to get to it, but its location served no purpose. After cutting it down, I jumped back over the fence with tree in hand. I stood by the roadside waving taxis down, but no one was stopping. Some would slow, but when they saw the tree, they hurried off. "Okay?" I thought. Where there is a will, there is a way. So, I stashed the tree over by the wall I had just jumped. I began waving my arms until the next taxi came and stopped. I looked at the guy and smiled; he had no idea what I was about to do. I opened all his doors and ran and grabbed the tree. Dashing toward the car, I shoved the tree into the back seat. I had him trapped now, and then as I closed the back two doors, I jumped into the front seat and pointed my finger the way toward my apartment. By now the driver was laughing and trying to talk with me, but all I could say was "Ting Bu Dong! Ting Bu Dong!" (I don't understand! I don't understand!)

Eventually, we made it to the front of my apartment complex. I exited the car, grabbed my tree, and drug it up four flights of steps. I placed the tree in the corner of my room and began the festive decorating. I couldn't wait to show Kenji. Then, I heard Kenji coming. As he walked in the door, he looked and said with a soft China accent, "Oh so pretty, where you get?" I said to him, "I found it down the road while riding bus." He looked at me and with a great big sigh said, "Oh no, oh no, you so crazy, always, always causing the problems. You will go to jail for cutting down the tree in China. I can't believe you so crazy." I couldn't help it. I laughed hysterically. "Kenji, this tree needs our love and it was getting any love where

I found it. So, you want to help me finish decorating the tree or not?" "Okay!" he said, "It will be the first time I ever decorate a tree for Christmas." What a great memory to have! Christmas was here and New Years was on the way. The party was a hit. I had a house full of guests and food everywhere. I could honestly say that this was one of my best Christmases ever, and I was ready to party all the way through the New Year. Xin nian yu kuai! (Shing ying quyla!) Happy New Year!

New Years, for most of us symbolizes the end of one era and the beginning of another. It's a time to reflect on what the past year held and what may come of the next, but mostly what my mind was thinking about during this time was my dear sweet Ally. I was really missing her. I missed her so badly that there was a hole in my heart and emptiness in my stomach. If I had only one wish, it would have been to hold her hand on Christmas morning and then spend the next few days cuddling in warm, fuzzy clothes by a fire, and when the midnight bell rang on New Years night, I would want to hold her sweet face in the palm of my hands and gently give her a long, soft, heart-felt kiss.

We had planned to talk to each other at midnight through phone, but it wasn't good enough for me. I wanted my new years and her new years to be together. I hated thinking we were apart for this special moment in time. I had always believed that how the New Year started predicted how it may end. And because of the distance between us, I feared she may just find love somewhere else, or at the least, my love may fade. Everyday we had sent love letters by email, and I had even mailed her a Christmas gift from China. The postage was more costly than the box of gifts I sent, but I was willing to break my tradition of no gift giving for the lady I loved.

Early Christmas day, I had a strange thing happen. When I first arrived in China, Ally had mailed me a letter and card for my birthday. My birthday is in October. She sent it in September to make sure it made it on time. By the end of October, the card had not made it, and so we both gave up on it ever making its way to my mail box. I told Kenji if I had one wish, it would be to spend Christmas day with her. After three months and after giving up on the postal service, Santa delivered a special gift. A call to my phone came in. A package had arrived in the dean's office. I figured my mom and some others had all pitched in to send me some American goodies. But guess what? The birthday card with Ally's photo had arrived Christmas day. What a great gift to receive, and as I opened the card and smelled the inside, it contained a hint of her scent and a lovely message. At that moment I wanted her there to hold and to love on. However, that wasn't going to happen, but at least I had my new best friend Kenji to celebrate with. And he would hold me, if I asked.

I missed home only because my love was far away. A few more months, I thought, and I would marry that girl, never to be without her again. I just needed this one last adventure before settling down, and since she was finishing her last year of graduate school, it just seemed to be perfectly planned. I would finish my year in China, she would graduate, and we could start a life together. The thing was, I hadn't quite told her yet that was my plan. I figured if I were going to commit my life to serving her, I would ask her hand in marriage in a most romantic way, and, believe me, I can be quite the charming man; but soon all these thoughts, all these things I had planned in my mind, would drastically change. A new song was playing and God again was taking the lead.

God again played with my destiny, and if I had a choice, I still don't know if I would relive what was about to come. Nevertheless, I can't change what some might say is already written. And, it's this part of the story that shakes me the most. It takes my breath from me every time I think about it. And now, to write it, well, I'm shaking here at the keyboard. It's hard to breathe, thinking about what I'm about to share with the world, but it's the truth, and it's truly amazing that I can share it. I just want to say if you've ever questioned the burning bush, the parting of the sea, Jonah living in a whale, walking on water, the rising of a dead Messiah, you're not alone in your doubt, but as sure as the sun rises, I'm here to say it's all true. I've experienced first hand the power of the one who conquered death. He came in my weakest moment and filled my life with a juice so sweet, a juice I like to call *Elephant Juice*.

## *Elephant Juice:*
## *Wild Elephant Valley*

After the Christmas season ended, so did the semester. I gave my final exams out to my students, and I was really glad to have experienced the teaching abroad program. My sum total of a being was being added to daily in my teaching experiences. As the winter break approached, my next plan was to use my five weeks off to explore Thailand, Cambodia, and Vietnam. However, the best part of my planned trip was the invitation Kenji had extended to me and our dear friend Sparkie. Kenji had asked if we would come to his village and stay with his family for the holiday. The Chinese get one week a year to visit family. For many, this may be the only time some of them see their wives, children, and parents. Not to skip ahead too much, but that year was the year of the great snow storm. Many died and many never could make it to see their families because they had never prepared for such a storm. The winter separated families, and many would have to wait another year before visiting their loved ones. As for me, though, I was headed south to lands with plenty of sunshine and tropical weather.

I told Kenji it would be a great honor to visit his village. I even was able to talk to his mother on the phone, and she seemed as happy as ever to invite this unknown white man into her home. I doubt she understood a word

I said, but I could tell she was excited about my coming. Kenji kept explaining over and over with his Chenglish, "My village very poor. My village never see white man before. It will be very happy for them, and I will baptize my grandfather. The whole village thinks he is crazy, but we will tell them about the God too." Kenji must have explained this to me a dozen times, and often he would say, "Look they already be scared when they see white man, so you don't scare them like you do me." I replied, "Kenji, I'm scaring every one of them, and I'm jumping in bed with your mom." Kenji would always say in return, "This is so crazy, maybe whole village leave when they see you." But the more Kenji talked about his village, the more lovely it came to be. He said over and over how poor they were, and I kept saying, "Brother, if I had only a rock to sleep on and thorn bush for shade, I would be the happiest man alive, because I was with him and the ones he loved the most." So, the trip was set.

January 20th I would catch a plane to Kunming where the sun was shining and the weather was that of Southern California. From Kunming I would head down to Thailand. From Thailand I would travel through Cambodia and then over into Vietnam. To end my trip I would come back into China to visit with Kenji and his village. Being in that village would be the high point of my trip. I never had a friend like Kenji, and I loved him very much. So the night before I left out, Kenji saw me off. Snow had fallen for days and my vacation was beginning. I was set for an adventure of a lifetime. Five weeks traveling through Asia had me on top of the world. The night of the 19th Kenji and I got a room together near the airport.

That evening he spent the whole night worrying about everything. He would say, "How you going to do this? My village is so hard to find. You will get lost. I know it. I know you get lost." Over and over, I tried to ease the mind of my over-worried friend, and to help I had Kenji just write the directions to his village in Mandarin, put his phone number on the paper, and if anything came up and I got lost, I would find a way to call. He kept saying, "It's so crazy. You go and travel by yourself and know nothing." I would say, "Kenji, I'm not alone. God is with me, don't worry."

"God is with me." If only I knew how surreal those words would become, I wonder what path I would have chosen. And so it was, January 20$^{th}$, I was up in the air. Though the snow was a foot deep in Wuhan, I was dressed in shorts and t-shirt. I knew once on the plane, my body would warm, and once off the plane, the weather would be in the high eighty's. Life was good. "But only if I had known?" Don't we all say this at times in our lives? At this point if I had known, I would have hugged my friend Kenji a little longer and a little tighter. I would have called family and said those three words that mean so much: "I Love You." But that's never the case. So, up in the air I was without a worry in the world.

I landed in Kunming, the capitol of the Yunan province. Yunan is known for all the different cultures of Asia kind of melting into one place. My first day, I just explored the new city, eating the food and relaxing on the sidewalks. I got a great massage. I was living the dream. The following day I went and visited this place that had a spectacular wonder of nature, a grassland of sort, with thousands of protruding giant grey stones jolting out of the earth, standing thirty to forty feet high. It was one of those sights that just marveled the mind. How and what in the world would cause such a landscape? There in the park I got to see a Chinese wedding take place, and of course that made me want Ally all the more, but for now I would just have to deal with the random phone calls and emails. Kind of weird, but the best feeling was when we kissed through the phone, of course I used my tongue, not so sure about her (JK). But that's neither here nor there. After seeing the sites around Kunming, I was excited to get down to Thailand. So, I ordered a ticket on a sleeper bus and headed to Xishuangbanna. It would be there I could check out the requirements for tourist visas. Looking at the map, I thought I would be in Xishuangbanna within a few hours; it turned out that I was on the longest, craziest bus ride in human history.

We must have spent fourteen to sixteen hours creeping up and down every valley in southwest China. Sometimes, we would be doing well over fifty mph on gravel curves, on the side of a steep mountain edge. Sometimes, I would peek out the window, and I could easily see that one wrong move and our bus would be tumbling down six thousand feet to the bottom of a tropical canyon. The wheels of the bus were only inches from sliding over at every point. To make it even more exciting, the road was built for two cars, but the bus took up the entire road, and we were taking curves, never knowing what was coming our way around the next bend. "Nuts!" I tell ya, "nuts!" But hey, this kind of excitement is what I live for. It was better than any rollercoaster ride I had ever been on. By the next day we had arrived in Xishuangnbanna. I was exhausted, so I went and dropped my pack in the cheapest hotel I could find.

After a shower and a meal, I sought out a tourist shop. Inside the shop, I found a trip known as the Diamond tour; it would start in China and go down the Mekong on the banks of Burma and into Thailand. The problem was the boat wasn't scheduled to leave for two days. Nevertheless, I went ahead and purchased the ticket and decided I would just hang around the area I was already in for a day or so. And that's exactly what I did. I found an Internet shop and sent out emails to a few people. In one particular email, I sent a letter of thanks to my Uncle Sam and Aunt Janet. They had sent me a care package and in that package was a pair of really comfortable shoes, and now that I was on my walk about, and I needed them. I can also remember saying in the letter, "If anything should happen to me, Sammy, know that I love and respect you very much." I'm not exactly sure if I had some premonition, but I did write those words, signed, of course, "love Jeremy."

With a day to kill before the boat trip, I googled things to do in the area, and in my search I came across Wild Elephant Valley. Little did I know my destiny was being written, and tragedy would soon strike. So, I went to some places and found out the next day I could take a trip out to the valley and view the wild elephants. The tourist shop had a painting on the wall that showed a bunch of people in a large tree-house observatory looking down into the valley at elephants grazing in the field. All my research and inquisitiveness told me I could just catch the bus tomorrow afternoon, get there sometime before dark, and view the elephants in a kind of sanctuary setting. And so I did exactly that. I bought a ticket for a ride out to Wild Elephant Valley. I was excited about the small trip I would take. With this planned and the boat trip coming in two days, it was time for rest. I figured I would go back to my small hotel room and just relax and enjoy some of the local food, and it was a peaceful evening.

January 24th, I woke early that day. The day seemed to have a normal feeling just as any other day would while traveling in foreign lands. I had planned to see something new and exciting. It would be one of those experiences I could later share with my future children, grandchildren, and certainly with my students. The day did seem to drag along pretty slow, however. The bus to Wild Elephant Valley was to depart around 1:30 or 2 o'clock that afternoon. The Internet said the best time to view the wild elephants was near dusk in the late afternoon. In my mind, I thought the bus ride would be thirty to forty-five minutes long. I figured myself and a hand full of other tourist would all be together. I figured we would exit together, buy our tickets, and go see the pachyderms. As I waited for the bus, I decided I would simply do nothing but have a few drinks and people watch. Eventually, it was time to board the charter. Come to find out, it wasn't so much a charter as it was an over-sized van with people piled upon people. As always I tried finding someone to speak English, and on this occasion there was no such person. So, I just sat back in my seat and waited to leave. As the bus rolled out, I wondered if this would even be worth seeing. I reckoned, I could go to a zoo and see the same thing, right? Turns out that's not the case; in fact, I was in for a great surprise.

Looking out from the bus window, I kept anticipating some kind of gated entrance, but something odd was going on. I thought we were a bus of tourists, but some would get off and others would get on. We made several stops in small villages to let people off and for others to get on. Some people would get off in the middle of nowhere and just take off walking through a field of crops. I also noticed a great number of banana trees along the roadside; they were growing everywhere. After a while my thirty minute bus ride turned into what seemed to be several hours. I had taken my ticket up to the driver and through body language and facial expressions he knew to tell me when it was my time to exit. To be double sure, I showed everyone on that bus my ticket, and I guessed that some would be going to the same place. After about two hours on the road, I started noticing elephant crossing signs. I thought, "Wow! I'm in deep now, and this ain't no zoo." Then, the bus came to a stop. The driver turned and pointed to me saying, "Zhe! Zhe!" Which translates to "Here, Here!" The door on the bus opened and I stood up to exit. I was a little confused because I was the only one getting out of my seat. As I got to the bus door, I just looked at the faces of the people who had stared at me for the past few hours and said what I knew best in Chinese, and that was, "Ting Bu Dong, Wo fei fungla" Which means "I don't understand, I've lost my mind." With that note, a few laughed, a few stared with uncertain glares, and others just seemed dazzled. I exited the bus alone.

Standing by the road all by myself, I noticed a little hut across the old bumpy highway, and a few signs. So, I walked over and began looking for a ticket booth. There wasn't one. There was a very small hotel, a long t-shirt booth with elephants t-shirts, and a historical writing of how Wild Elephant Valley came to be. There were pictures of the elephants playing in the river that wound through the jungle landscape. The photos gave the impression that the creatures were harmless and peaceful. If I remember correctly, the Asian elephants were brought into that area to rid the jungle of the tigers that were overpopulating the countryside. There were thirty-three known wild elephants roaming the area. I still couldn't believe a person could just catch a bus and get off at any point in the jungle and have elephants appear at anytime. The few Chinese people that were in the area sold t-shirts and snack foods, and there was one guy who had a small black bear on a leash and another man who stood above a pit where a tiger ran in circles at the bottom of a concrete pit. Besides these people, there were no others. Looking at each of them, I started saying "Donsha? Donsha?" (Elephant? Elephant?) They all had the same reaction and pointed toward the path that was cut through the jungle. So, I followed their directions.

It was well after four o'clock, and if I were going to get to that tree house overlooking the valley, I needed to hoof it fast. The painting the tourist shop portrayed showed a picture of 'many' tourists looking over a deep valley with elephants way down at the bottom. But, I think this must have been some sort of hoax, or possibly, I was the last of the tourists. I walked hard and fast. One little sign did catch my eye, and it read, "Be Careful Elephants May Appear On Path Suddenly." Looking to the right of the little sign, I noticed a huge footprint about three feet in diameter. It hit me then. I was there in the jungle, and not only was I there alone, but at anytime a wild elephants could walk out in front of me at any time. However, I really never expected it to happen. Nevertheless, I began walking as hard and fast as I could down the path. I was still convinced that there was a tree house full of tourists somewhere at the end of the path. About an hour later, I reached the end. I noticed some raised bungalows made out of metal and some straw hut dwellings in the trees. I also saw a few Chinese men sitting at a table playing cards. As I tried to grasp all that was going on, I realized that the huts were these people's homes. The purpose of the tree houses was so the elephants didn't trample over them. Standing on the raised bridge were three people. They weren't Chinese, so I figured they were tourists, and I was hoping they spoke some English.

I approached the two guys and the girl and asked "English?" The lady answered, "Yes, a little" My next question, "Have you seen any elephants?" "No," she replied, "We have been here all day. We have this bungalow to sleep in, and we are waiting to see if they come through here tonight. You can stay with us if you would like." I thought about it for second, and decided, "Nah, I'm just going to get out of here. Who knows if the elephants will come through or not? Thanks for the invite but I got a boat to catch to Thailand in the morning." So, I told them bye and wished them happy journeys.

The next thought as I turned and started my trek back toward civilization left me questioning how I would actually get back into the city, being so far out. I didn't want to get caught in the jungle after dark, but I had come so far to see these wild animals. One more chance I hoped. I walked over to the jungle dwelling Asian men who were playing some sort of card game and I asked, "Dansha?" They turned and with their palms open to the air and with their body language, they suggested, "Who Knows?" They shrugged their shoulders and returned to playing the card game. With that being the case, my mind told me to it was now time to leave. Besides, I could ride elephants in Thailand and that sounded much more adventurist.

I began to march out. I noticed some colorfully dressed Chinese men heading down the path that led to the entrance. I decided I would follow them. To this day I still wonder what their purpose was; nevertheless, I was going to stay up with them as they knew the way out. But then along the way, I wanted to stop for some pictures. I remember a large monkey just chillin by the path. I found him quite intriguing and worth taking pictures of. Then, there were the massive tropical trees and wild plants of the forest all vibrant, green, and lush. I wanted to capture it all on my little digital camera, and before I realized it the guys I was going to walk along with had disappeared into the jungle. I realized darkness would soon come, and I began walking with great stride. I didn't want to get caught in that area with no light in the sky and chance having to sleep in the forest. I had a bed just a few hours away, and I was determined to get back to the city.

I walked quickly down the path. I came back across a bamboo bridge I had crossed earlier. The small spongy bridge stood over a small, brown-stained, muggy river that wound all throughout the jungle valley. On that bridge, I decided to take a video for those who might be interested in my journey. In the video I say, "Hey everyone, thought I would see some wild elephants here in the jungle, but apparently I'm not going to. Maybe in Thailand we can ride an elephant, but for now I'm signing off." I took the camera and scrolled around at what I was viewing. While doing so, I narrated my thoughts, "This is what the jungle looks like, pretty cool, but weird." Then, I point the camera at myself, and with big smile, I said, "Until the next time, this is Jeremy, signing off."

What happened next can only stretch your faith. If you have ever questioned God and the existence of supernatural powers, hold onto your seats because I'm here to tell you, God is real, and miracles do happen. In my own metaphorical way, I was about to walk on water, with Christ holding my hand. I was raised from the dead. I became the crippled man who was healed by amazing love, the deaf who suddenly could hear, the blind who could see. I didn't know it then, but now I understand why David danced for Jesus. And now when I sing, I sing with a real deep joy. His power is unbelievable. I had gone through many hells before this day, but I never thought I was important enough to be a chosen child of

God, a man who can say "My life is a miracle. I have so many sins, more than I'll ever admit in any of my writings or ever admit to any one person. God knows what a wretched person I really am. Yet, he still loves me." Readers this same love and supernatural being wants more than anything to hold you in His arms and give you the peace and security we all desire. All we have to do is listen to the soft voice that says, "Never will I leave, nor forsake you."

Looking back to that moment in life is very painful for me. In retrospect, I was trying to bargain with God. I was trying to cover my sins with good deeds. I was doing those deeds in the name of God, trying to manipulate him with my own thoughts. Truth is, I was as sinful as ever before. I was still a harlot at heart, a man of self desires, a person who thought of himself first and just pretended to carry his cross. I was a fake. I did believe and I was baptized. But looking back now, I thought forgiveness was given at baptism and so whatever the case afterward, grace would cover me. My humanity excuse was simply a cop-out. Yet, the scriptures screamed, "Brothers, I ask you why should we go on sinning...?" Now, I give you the juice...

## *Elephant Juice: Mercy*

After shooting the video from the bamboo bridge, I noticed the colorful Chinese people had gone far from my sight. I began to hurry out; for fear that darkness would soon come over me. I came around a bend and realized I was near the place where I had first entered. A sigh of relief, I didn't want to be caught in the jungle after dark, especially considering I was going to have to hitch-hike my way back to the city. Then, a sudden loud trumpet sound screamed through the forest, "Heernnn!" Then, another loud sound screamed, "Herrrnnn!" There in the distance they stood. I was taken back, I was breathlessly in awe. There were several wild elephants approximately fifty yards in front of me. They were eating the tops out of the banana trees, and suddenly I decided to become Mr. Discovery channel. I wanted to capture this moment. I wanted to get closer. I was as deep in this moment as any moment of my life. With camera set to video, I slowly began walking up to the gi-normous animals. I was there, I was really there. I was a part of nature at its best. It was like I had traveled back in time. I felt like a well dressed caveman, with all the future technology in hand. I would soon share with the world my new discovery. Step by step, I got closer and closer. I was easy going and very light footed. One wrong move and they might run off. My heart raced with excitement as I watched them through the camera screen.

To the right two of the elephants began trotting toward the other three. The mother and father elephant stood staring with calm eyes, and the baby was tucked between the two. The excitement was wonderful and exhilarating. My heart pounded with excitement. Next thing I knew, I was walking with the giants. I was only an arms reach away. Still with video rolling, I captured the whole scene. One by one they started walking by me. The first passed by, walking directly in front of me, moving from my right to my left. I watched its tail go by. Then, number two followed suit, and they were all marching in one line. I was overwhelmed with emotion. The video images all of the sudden lost importance. I was in the moment; I wanted to touch these ancient creatures. In this moment, I was the envy of myself. Then, as the second elephant was almost past and third was about to walk by, I decided to reach out and touch the back leg of the second one. If I didn't do it now, they would all soon be out of my reach and off into the jungle. They seemed so docile, like huge, gentle giants. No fear could be read in the mannerism of the pachyderms. I reached to turn off my camera, but before I could hit the 'off' button, the four adult elephants turned toward me simultaneously and in sync began trotting toward me. They were flickering there trunks at my head and sounding their trumpets loudly. "Herrrrnnn! Herrrnnn!" screamed the giants.

Calmly, I began taking huge steps backwards as they charged me. Head to head with the largest of the four, I began saying with a nervous, fearful, gentle voice, "No, no, no, no, no." I spread my arms out as to surrender to the giant beings, stating I come in peace. My backward trot became faster and faster, and their pace was also increasing. My heart was pounding through my chest. I knew I was in big trouble, but still I didn't think they really wanted to hurt me; so, I continued to try and calm them by slowly and calmly repeating, "No, no, no." But it was useless; the Chinese elephants just didn't understand English. They were now loudly trumping toward me. It was definite; they were out to kill me. Still stepping backwards, I began thinking about escape routes. I looked right and left, but nothing came to mind. They all marched toward me standing side by side, each standing eight to twelve feet tall and as wide as a school bus. I was in deep trouble. With each trump toward me their speed increased. And their trumpets screamed louder and louder, "HEEERRRRRN! HEEERRRNN! HEEEERRRRRNNN!"

I looked around for a final escape route, I realized there was no hole to jump into, and there was no way to out run the creatures or out juke them. I thought about climbing a tree, but I realized with my first leap they would easily knock me down. I could in no way leap higher than their head in one thrusting leap. I fought the desire to turn and run. As long as I had them in my sight, I might have a chance. All I could imagine was one knocking me over the head with it's' trunk and stomping all over me. Then the deer hunter instinct kicked in. I knew that deer saw things in shades of blue and gray. And at that point, I hoped that they, the elephants, were also colorblind; and if it were so, I could perhaps jump into a bush or behind a tree and they could possibly pass me by as I blended in with the landscape. So, with a few faster, higher steps backwards, I made a leaping dash behind a huge tree and hugged it, trying to camouflage myself quickly. "Could this work?"

Using my peripherals, I saw two pass by on the left side. A little relief came. Then, looking right out the corner of my eyes, I saw another one coming around as if he too would pass me by, but where was number four? The biggest of the four was just a split second ago head to head with me. Yet, he hadn't passed by. The tree I hugged had a split in it, a 'Y' split right above my head. I looked up and through the 'Y,' and there was the fourth one. Standing on its back two feet, sixteen to eighteen feet tall, 12,000 pounds, with its two legs in striking position and its trunk pointed toward the heavens, it let out a loud, terrifying, trumpet sound, "HERRRRRRRNNNNN!" Then, with its front two feet and with all its crushing might, WAM! It drilled the tree with both feet. It was trying to knock the tree down on me. I let out a scream. I'm sure was heard throughout the entire valley, "NOOOOOO!!!" I turned to my left and realized that the two that had passed on the left side had turned back in toward me and were charging right at me full speed. I then juked to the right, but before I could even turn my head, the one that had gone to my right drilled me with its trunk. WAM! I went flying through the air like a ragdoll. Then, the one behind the tree stepped in and began romping me with it's' trunk and kicking me, as did the other three. I was trapped; they had me boxed in on all four sides. I was being kicked and trunked and tossed about like a soccerball. The power of these animals was tremendous. I'm a two-hundred fifty pound man, and to them it was like I was a small beach ball being kicked in every direction. In fact, I never recall my feet ever touching the ground. And to this day, I can still feel the toughness of their skin. My next instinct was to cover my head and ball up as tight as possible protecting my head and face. Up to this point, the blows had not really hurt me, but what happened next would leave me broken and crushed. My life was surely coming to an end.

The largest of the four elephants, the one that had tried to knock the tree over on me, was now at my back. I know this and every detail because I never lost consciousness throughout the whole situation. I was aware of every single blow and kick and which of the four was doing what, but the oddest thing happened next. In fact, it is still unbelievable, something I never imagined possible. Standing behind me, the largest elephant took its trunk and threw it over my head, reaching over me and grabbing me under my crotch, and with one swift move, it just scooped me up into its mouth and bit me. I heard my body crackle from bottom to top, it was a loud crunch. I heard my bones crush and felt them all crumble inside me. It became dark, inside its mouth, and my head was now folded between my knees. The only part that dangled out of its mouth was the lower extremities of my legs; from the knees down both legs straddled each side of the trunk. My life was over, and I knew it.

It's funny how the mind works in tragedy, and the thoughts running through my mind were oddly rational. My first thought was simply, "These things eat plants?"

My next thought was the digestive process, and in my imagination, I envisioned my shoe stuck in elephant dung, "crazy huh?" But it's the truth. Next, I thought about all my sins, even the ones I had committed earlier in the day and the previous days. And at that point, all I had left to say was, "God, forgive me; I'm a sinner." Do you believe in miracles? Is it possible to walk on water? Can the blind be healed? Can a burning bush speak to man? Can water be turned to wine? Can death be conquered? Was the messiah raised from the tomb? The answer, the answer has to be "Yes."

The split second I prayed that prayer for forgiveness, I mean the very split-second I got the word 'sinner' out of my mind, the elephant opened its mouth and spit me out. I came crushing down on the earth's canvas, landing directly on my left side. Still completely conscious, I looked up and over my right shoulder, I saw the giant's right front foot come smashing down on me; it squished me in like silly-putty. The circumference of the elephant's foot extended from the top of my head down below my waist line. Specialists in the field of elephants say the impact of a stomp can exert a force of 1,000 pounds. Can you imagine 1,000 pounds crashing down on a person? The stomp squished me in, and when it lifted its foot off me, the gravity bounced me onto my back. I looked up with death inevitably coming over my soul. I saw its' right foot once again lifted, ready to finish me off with a second crushing stomp. And that's exactly what I wanted it to do. I thought, "Finish me!"

## *Elephant Juice: There's a Stirring*

The last part of the previous chapter just brought me to my knees. I am weeping today as I write this letter to you all. Though the foot of the elephant was raised and ready to complete my demise, and my mind was thinking "Finish me!" I guess my heart had a different thought, "If-only I could live one more day." 'If-only'... right? We all say this from time to time in life. And it's those "ifs" that can drive us to our wit's end, but on that final day when we take our last breath, the surrealness of 'if-only' becomes very intense.

People often say live your life like it was your last day on earth. I doubt seriously anyone ever truly does this, maybe those who are in a situation where their days are numbered, maybe those on death row or those who have a terminal illness or disease. Just maybe those people live as if their living their last day. But most of us zoom through life without thinking about this much. We simply rise in the morning and head out the door to take on life. We never expect to have a herd of elephants attack us. We never expect death to find us in our jungle of life. We just never know when our lives will end. The only thing we are certain of is that everyone will die. And it's the afterlife that becomes so intriguing. It's the answer to our mystery we all wish we knew, but then, maybe then, life wouldn't be so beautiful.

Looking back, I can see the giant beast place its right foot gently and directly beside my head. Only inches from my face was the foot that could have crushed death into my being. Just before, I was sure his foot was going to come crashing down on me a second time and finish me off. However, for whatever reason, the elephant made an odd choice. Instead of stomping me, his leg came to a pause and then gently he put his foot to the left of my head. I looked up at the beast as one leg was to the right of my body and the other directly to left of my head. Its' trunk was dangling there above my body. The earth stood still and silence filled the air as I looked into the eyes of the beast that just sought to kill me. I noticed a very sad look about it. I thought "Is that it?" The elephant sniffed me for a second, and then, just like that all the elephants at once turned and began walking away, leaving me as food for the rest of what might search out an evening snack. As I watched them walk slowly away, I felt mangled and twisted. I couldn't move anything except my right arm. I noticed my shoe setting only a few inches from head, and I felt the other shoe was also missing. Those creatures literally knocked me out of my shoes. "Wow! What great power!" Then, as I tried to comfort myself for death's arrival, I realized I was broken and could not move. I looked down and saw the damage done.

All my life I had led a destructive lifestyle, partying like it was 1999. and only a short while back was I brought into the light. I looked down and my intestines were bulging through my shirt on my left side. They looked just like they did in the biology books. They were grouped together in about the size of a grapefruit. Blood soaked my shirt, and I was all alone. A lot of thoughts go through the mind of a dying man. Some were shared in my introduction, but there were so many more. In the beginning this book, I did not feel it necessary to share openly all my thoughts. However, I'm now at peace with the situation and will elaborate on the thoughts of a dying man. Or at least what it was like for me. It's not an easy thing to write. It is not an easy thing to confess. I have many shortcomings. And, I guess if I had a death bed confession, this might be what it would sound like.

Lying there in a pool of my own blood, I thought back on all the things that I had done in life. I wasn't at first thinking about my entire life's journey but rather what I had done just the day before, and the week before and the month before. All the choices I had recently made were running through my head over and over again. I thought about all the sins that may separate my soul from God. I thought about how wicked I truly was. I thought my destiny might end up in darkness. Then, my mind swayed to the thought of heaven. The thought of grace, the thought of Christ and his blood began to fill my mind. I was there knocking on heavens door, begging for the light to come and greet me. Gasping for air, I began praying. "Please God, have mercy on me. Please, father, bring me comfort, I'm hurt and dying. I just want the pain to go away."

God had found me long ago. He had put many paths before me, and I chose the wrong doors in most cases. My curiosity and desire to be filled with every fleshly experience had often separated me from God. There is such a dark loneliness in that separation. My life would only be filled with emptiness after the flesh was satisfied by its evil desires. But this day, this certain day, the path I was on in Wild Elephant Valley would set me before his throne. My judgment was coming, and I had no idea my life was about to change forever. Before I move any further, I feel the need to offer a prayer. I would ask that you listen to my confession, listen to my truths as I pray in writing, please pray for me, this is not the easiest thing to let the world know, but it's honest and truthful: This is who I am:

"My God, my father, I'm a wicked, selfish, filthy being. I am only cleansed by your blood. I am only given hope because I crucified you and you still loved me. I took the hammer in my hand and drove the nails through your wrists and through your feet. I pounded the nails over and over through your flesh. I spat upon your face and mocked your holy name. And I did so because I hated being loved by someone I couldn't understand. My father, I am truly sorry for nailing you to that cross. But sometimes I can't help myself. I give you the excuse that I am human, and sometimes, I think you should do as I want you to do instead of my doing as you asked me to do. Often I have prayed, 'Your will be done, not mine,' but you know my heart. You know I still want my will; it's so hard to surrender myself totally to you. Even now as you have come into my life and changed me forever. I still want my ways. God, I feel horrible inside for being so very selfish. I really do want to give my all to you, but my flesh just won't allow me, so I'm still stuck here on your earth, following a path that does somehow get more and more narrow. God, you have given me so much. I see your eyes and pain as you lay bleeding with the crown of thorns that I smashed onto your head, and yet, I still hear your soft voice repeating, "I love you, I love you, I love you." Yet, I smirk and I say, "If you do love me, then let me do as I please and still allow me to enter your gates." But then a reality comes about my spirit; I can't have the best of both worlds. Those times I stole from others, you forgave me. Those lies I told to get my way, you stood before the father and said, "He doesn't understand. Please, father, give him another chance." And then, after you said this, I went and entered the beds of those prostitutes and defiled your temple, only to have a moment of satisfaction, and yet, you still loved me. I've cursed you. I've yelled numerous times, "Why God? Why do you love me!" This war within is too much to bear sometimes. Why not do away with me and give me what I deserve? But even as I dare you to do so, you still say, "I love you. You are my son. I will not forsake you." Father God, Holy Spirit, Jesus, Hallelujah! You are the best friend I'll ever have and ever could have, and this, I know this for sure. And for your sacrifice, I am selfishly thankful. But still I feel unworthy. As a man you came to earth. Your spirit of valor will not even let a low-life as myself fall into the grips of the evil one, and I can't see why. I can only say thank you for hope. Thank you for loving me, and please help me to do the same. Help me crucify my flesh. You were broken to heal the desperate. By your stripes, we are forgiven. By your broken body, we have absolute hope. Thank you for breaking me and for a hint of what suffering is. Thank you for this journey called life. And because of your life, I do sometimes sigh peaceful breaths. Be with me, oh Lord, and keep that stirring deep within me. I need you, and I am nothing without you. You are my all in all. This is my prayer, these are my truths, and this is my confession." Amen.

Lying on the jungle floor, my breath became shallow. I then realized, I did have some hope, I did have a shot at heaven. I thought it was possible that God may just shove my face into the pits of hell. He may just give me a glimpse of what grace saved me from. Then, maybe I would appreciate heaven and His love for his children a little more.

So many thoughts of what may happen swayed from hell to heaven. Then a song came to mind. I had just learned it a few months back. I was told by my friend Adam that it was a funeral song and now it fit perfectly into my life. So, with hope and desperation, I began singing in a deep, shallow, fading voice...

"There's a stirring deep within me, could it be my time has come? When I'll see my gracious savior, face to face when all is done.
Is that his voice I am hearing? Come away my precious one. Is he calling me? Is he calling me?
I will rise up, rise up, and I'll bow down, lay my crown at his precious wounded feet. There's a stirring deep within me."

As I ended this song, no light came through the trees to lift my soul from its shell. I knew my life was at its end, and I was ready to call it quits. I had suffered long enough. I thought all a dying man could think. It was time to meet my maker. I decided to quicken the dying process. If God weren't coming to me, I would go ahead and end my pain, and end my life.

## *Elephant Juice: Suicide*

Many of us come to the thought of ending our own lives. Some deny the thought ever existed, those people either have it too easy, or maybe they are stronger than the rest of us. Many just can't deal with life circumstances. And that day when I was lying on the jungle floor destined for death, I figured speeding up the process was the right thing to do. Often we use the phrase, 'pull the plug,' and that's got to be one of the hardest things to say. Basically, one just gives up. The thought of living any longer just becomes exhausting and painful, and that's exactly how I felt. I was ready to accept my fate, whatever it might be? The pain was too much.

I reached down with my right hand and cupped my intestines. They were warm, gooey and slimy. I decided the best way to end the suffering was to yank them out of the way and reach in the deep, bleeding gash under my ribs and disconnect my heart. I would do so on the count of three with one fluid motion. On with death!

"One… (breathe) two… (deep breath, hand slightly gripping the intestines) and (hesitantly) thr…" … "Hey!" Sounded a hidden voice in the forest. "Was it another person?" I thought. And so, I murmured in a low whispering voice, "Hhh, hhh, hhhey." But my voice was too low. I tried again, "Hhhelp, hhhelp" I cried in a low whisper.

But still, I had no voice. My lungs were crushed, and I couldn't speak. No sound would break through my wind pipes. I was sure I had heard a human voice, so one more time sounded out. With every ounce of air, I oohed. "Oooh, Oooh." And yes, a response echoed from the bush, "Oooh, Oooh." I looked to my right and there stood the elephants. Still to this day I see their eyes, their demeanor saddened. They just mauled me, beating and stomping me from every angle. Yet, I think they felt sorrow for following their instincts. They just did what was natural. It was I who made the wrong choice of interrupting their territory. Maybe I should have done more research, but what's done is done. I made a choice and they chose to attack. And now, I was lying on the jungle floor dying crying out to the voice in the wilderness. Would he ever find me? Did he see the elephants and was he afraid to come any closer? To these questions, I still don't know the answer. Yet, in the midst of my drowning, God came looking for me again. He came as a voice in the wilderness.

I looked to my right, and I noticed the beasts walking even further away. And out of the darkening jungle the voice once again came, "Oooh, oooh" And with this last hope of being found and with all I had and all I could gander up, I let out a yelp, "Oooh! Oooh! Oooh! Help! Help! Help! Help! Oooh! Help! Help! Help! Oooh! Help! Help! Help!" I didn't care at that moment if the man found me or the beasts were startled enough to come back and finish me off. All I knew was something had to happen.

Then, a shadow popped out behind a tree. The elephants were now at least a half a football field away, and I lifted my right arm and waved to the shadow. A small Chinese man came running my way. When he approached me, he looked down and saw the blood and guts, and with shock he screamed, "AHHH!" He then turned the other way and took off running. I was as shocked as he was. What was so horrible? Why didn't he come and hold me in his arms or at least hold my hand? All sorts of thoughts zipped through my mind. Then, I saw him and another reappear. He hadn't left me; he just went to get more help.

It's funny; I was ready to die and was glad that someone was there to see me off. Yet, in another's mind, I wasn't dead yet, and he was going to do all he could to keep me alive. The two men tried to lift me from the ground. As they raised my torso my intestines all drooped down. I was too heavy for the two of them and the pain was escalating. I motioned with my head and body language, "Down! Down!" They understood and gently laid me back down. It was quite a relief. But they were not finished yet. One took off running through the jungle, and before I knew it, I saw two or three more men coming my way carrying a huge hammock-like structure. The structure was made from long bamboo poles and a dark green army blanket. They sat the make-shift gurney directly beside my body. Next, they all together lifted me onto the structure. Then two stood at my feet and two at my head and another in the center and all at once they tried elevating me, but still I was too heavy and they were not balanced. My body was aching. I still knew death was coming, but the most memorable thing was the thirst and the heat.

As the jungle dwellers quickened themselves and scurried about the area looking for more hands to help carry me. I was overwhelmed by fever and thirst. I had never been so thirsty. The thirst I was suffering from was more intense than I could ever explain. I had been miles into the desert of Utah, out of water, in the hot July sun, and that was nothing compared to this. I was dehydrated and fading quickly. I looked to the right and saw my water bottle, and with my right hand and finger, I pointed directly to the water bottle and in their on language I begged for it, "Shway, Shway!" They refused my deep desperate desire. Again I begged and pointed, "Shway, Shway!" and again they refused and told me no, "booya, booya." As I lay there, my mind drifted to the scriptures.

I began thinking back on Jesus' last moments, and I remembered his last words. Beaten publicly, whipped with spikes, kicked, angrily punched, spit upon, thorns smashed onto his head, nailed and crucified to a cross, Jesus had lost an incredible amount of blood. Humiliated and sweating tears of blood, he endured more than any of us can imagine. Then the words He uttered echoed into my soul. He simply said, "I'm thirsty." And after that, he stated, "It is finished." Putting all of this in perspective, I feel certain the Scripture was accurate but our reading of it may be a little dry. I think Mel Gibson's *The Passion* was right on in the goriness of what Jesus went through. And I'm certain his thirst was similar to what I was experiencing there in the jungle. However, I deserved my punishment. And He? Well, He was perfect, and 'we' crucified Him. In that moment Jesus was more real than ever before.

Christ' humanity became all the more evident to me in this moment of despair. I am sure that He didn't simply say in a monotone voice, "I'm thirsty." If I were to guess, I bet Jesus was panting and in a deep, shallow, desperate, whispering cry, said something more in the tune of "Water, wa-wa-water, please water, I'm thirsty, water." And then as we mocked him with old wine placed on a sponge and teased his lips with something that could never satisfy human thirst, He realized His human life was over, and then he said reluctantly and humbly, "It is finished." His human body died.

Taking all this into account, I knew for sure my minutes were numbered. I gave myself five at best. Yet, I still noticed the Chinese jungle-men gathering more and more people. I noticed several of the men forming a line to the left of me and then another group forming a line to the right. One man with glasses looked down on my broken body. And, I was still trying to beg for water. I didn't understand what his exact words were, but I knew none of them were going to hand me the drop of water I cried for. I decided it was time to say my last words. I had not learned very much of the Chinese language, but I had learned enough to say what was most important. And so, with my mind focused on my last words, and my heart crying out for a plea of mercy, "Come Lord, come now." I began repeating with a loud, whispering voice, "Ye-su ai ni! Ye-su ai ni!" I don't know how or where I got the voice to sound loudly from my lips, over and over, louder and louder, I exclaimed, "Ye-su ai ni! Ye-su ai ni! Ye-su ai ni!" For several minutes, I repeated this phrase, "Jesus loves you! Jesus loves you!" In a certain way it was my last cry for forgiveness. Then, all at once, something extraordinary happened within me.

With seven men on each side of me, they all at once lifted me up on their shoulders. The bamboo poles of the make-shift stretcher rested on their shoulders and they began marching me out of the jungle. Of all the spiritual moments I had experienced in life, this was the pinnacle of them all. I went from staring up in the sky through the darkening, jungle canopy hoping for the light of heaven to shine down upon me. I imagined my soul being lifted from my body and into the sky. And in a split second, that hope of heaven changed to a strange, awkward 'knowingness' that I was not to die this day. I remember specifically thinking, "Damn it, I'm not going to die."

Following this thought, came all the other humanity factors I would endure. I thought, "At the least, I will be handicapped. I'm probably never going to walk, and that sucks. From the waist down nothing will work. So that means, I'm never going to have sex and that really sucks." Adding to this thought was, "I'm never going to have children of my own, and that even sucks more. And, I am probably pretty much useless as a human being, so, what will I do?" Ally, then entered my mind; "I can't do anything for her anymore," and I was sure that the stomp of the elephant disfigured my face, so now I would be ashamed to be seen in public. So, "what would come of me? What would I do with this damaged body?"

So many speculations ran through my mind as they continued marching me out of the jungle.

"Could I tell my story and have someone else write it? Would my story become a best seller?" Positive thoughts began replacing the negative thoughts. I wasn't dead yet, and a miraculous thing was taking place. God had kept me alive for some reason, and I knew the future held something great for me. And then it hit me. I could be shot-put champion in the Special Olympics. I actually pictured myself in a tight red spandex Olympic-style suit, with the number 777 placed on my chest. I saw myself throwing the shot-put with my one good right arm. I saw myself determined and smiling, receiving a gold medal. With that thought, I breathed a sigh of relief. I still had purpose, but the pain was not wavering and the nearest city and hospital were still hours away. And to my surprise, I noticed my rescuers were headed in a different direction than the way I had entered the jungle path. Why this way? And why were they climbing me up a steep embankment. The path to the highway was straight ahead and level. Confusion sunk in. I wondered, "Where are they taking me?" Possibly, I was wrong. Possibly, I was still going to die. Yet, I was sure of that feeling, "Be calm my son, I am with you."

## *Elephant Juice:*
## *I Am, My Brother's Keeper*

Up through the valley the men carried me, and once we topped the hill an old truck was backed and waiting to transport my carcass to its next destination. It was dark, but the moon lit sky shined enough of that I can recall the color of the truck was blue. It had wooden planks built up over the bed, kind of like a garbage truck. In fact, it looked just like the truck from the old show *Sanford and Son*. Nevertheless, they loaded me in the back, and several of them jumped in the bed with me. The man with the glasses was holding my hand and as the breeze blew over the cab onto my fevered face, I closed my eyes in relief. I can easily recall the feeling of that breeze. It was refreshing and soothing. Then, the man holding my hand began patting my face to wake me up. I couldn't explain that I wasn't trying to sleep or die. I knew I wasn't going to die at this point. I was just enjoying the cool breeze on my hot face, but he refused to let me close my eyes. With a grin, I looked at him and showed deep appreciation for his concern. I believe he felt my thankfulness. Then, another obstacle rolled through my mind: the road this truck was on wasn't complete. I saw this highway running parallel to the road that brought me into the Wild Elephant Valley. So, what would happen when we reached the barricades?

The truck suddenly came to a quick halt. The men jumped quickly out and moved to the front of the truck. We encountered a barricade. I heard them all working together to move the structure out of the way. "E-R-Sun... hhhutttt," a loud grunt followed. Then, as quickly as they had jumped out of the truck, they hopped right back in. The same man held my hand again and comforted me, and then the next barricade. And again they jumped out, and I heard the same count, "E-R-Sun" and a loud grunt followed. They were counting "one-two-three" and then moving whatever obstacles stood in the way. Eventually, we came to a crossroad. I saw many flashing red lights and what seemed to be the top of a toll passage. Suddenly, I came sliding out of the pick-up truck and was quickly placed on a small stretcher. They placed me inside a small popsicle-sized ambulance. My guess was that someone radioed ahead and had the medical team meet us at the toll. The ambulance was very small, and several nurses with their white masks and old fashioned paper-white nurse caps tried to strap me in, and place an IV into my arms. But, I was large, and I have rolling veins, and they did not succeed. I guess it was a likelihood that I may have been their largest patient ever, especially considering I was too large to strap in, and they had to hold my stretcher and body in place by hand inside the ambulance. Next, they started the count down, "Fifty-five ...forty-five ... thirty-five ...ten ... five." I understood that they were counting the minutes before we would arrive at the hospital.

Pulling into the ER was strange. I could see the buildings that I had passed earlier that day, and everything that had happened in the past few hours seemed unreal. As they pulled me out of the ambulance, a great crowd of people circled around me and lights were flashing everywhere. The nurses and doctors quickly pushed me through the crowd and into a concrete block room. One doctor came and looked down at me and asked, "Where is your passport?" I thought, "What in the world are you talking about? Get me fixed; worry about that stuff later!" However, I answered with a shallow breath, "It's in the jungle with the rest of my stuff. Can I please get something for pain?" "Oh yes, yes." he replied. He then proceeded to the foot of the small bed along with the rest of the medical team. The obvious injury was my abdomen where the intestines were bulging through my shirt. I knew it was worse than what they were seeing. I had felt some of my other innards fall out underneath my shirt when the first two Chinese men tried to lift me. One of the doctors lifted the right side of my shirt and all at once they had the same exact reaction, "Ooooh." I exclaimed very matter-of-factly, "Ooooh yea, pain medicine." Then, like a switch, I was out.

Anesthesia was administered and they performed many life saving operations through-out the night. My lungs had collapsed, nine ribs were crushed, my heart was contused, my stomach was punctured, my shoulder was busted, and my rotator cuff had popped out of place. My lower back was broken. I was disemboweled. I had nerve damage all around, but the most serious injuries were internal. I had lost a lot of blood in those four hours before reaching the hospital. All night the surgeons did everything they could to stabilize me, until finally, they ran out of resources. One report stated that twenty-nine surgeries were performed that one night. I was hooked up to monitors and had tubes coming in and out of my stomach, lungs, and chest. I was on an oxygen machine and had the discomfort of a catheter inserted into my penis. Talk about a hard life, this was one hell of a fight, and the funny thing is, this was just round one. The battle for survival was being fought. Yet, my God, my Lord, my soul's keeper stood before me with his angels, and began healing me in so many ways.

I was truly broken in every way a life could be broken. I was physically destroyed, emotionally in need, spiritually dying, and mentally unprepared for the trial and fight I was about to embark on. Just like in the Hollywood films, everything was pitch black as I came to consciousness from the numerous surgical procedures. It was early morning. I heard the heart monitor. "Beep… beep… beep… beep… beep," the monitor was in perfect rhythm with the beat of my heart. With my eyes clinched shut, I began thinking, "What's next? Where exactly am I? What will happen when I open my eyes? Am I alone? What will I see?" Truth is, I was afraid to open my eyes. For the first time, I didn't like the unknown. Then, as the heart monitor kept sounding out, "beep… beep… beep… beep," my eyes slowly opened, and there he was. Holding my hand against his forehead, praying over my body in a very dimly lit room, Kenji looked at my face, he smiled, and in the sweetest Chinese voice I had ever heard, he spoke these words, "It's okay, I will be with you til the end, no matter what." These were the words of Jesus. My heart shattered.

Truly at this moment, the love of God came over me like a mighty rushing wind. A love deeper than any ocean, wider than any galaxy and more powerful than any storm, the healing of my body, mind and soul could now begin. The power of these words, "I will be with you til' the end," was now an absolute truth for me. The power of Christ love I will never comprehend, and just like that my fears were gone. Kenji, my brother from a different mother, came to shine the light. He was poor china-man, and he risked his livelihood to do what Jesus asks us all to do. Love with the love of God, and do so without fear. Kenji had come across the country leaving all his own worries behind. He was the voice of Christ, and I will forever be grateful for his sacrificial love. Kenji is my favorite part of the whole story. Kenji, my brother, my friend, gave me the motivation for a desperately needed hope, a hope that resides in his heart of gold, and that hope is the spirit of God, a pure and Holy Spirit. It's the greatest gift any soul can receive and now my doubts were answered. Christ does fill His people with a spirit of love, and Kenji became the evidence that showed me what it meant to be a brother in Christ. Worship is self-sacrifice. We are our brother's keepers.

## *Elephant Juice:*
## *The Death Chamber*

Kenji smiled upon me with a tear rolling down his cheek, and another voice sounded behind him. Tyler, my American buddy, had also flown in. He was from Missouri and had been in China for several years. Tyler is a straight up guy. He doesn't sugar coat anything, and I love that about him. His words were humorous. He said, with a southern, country accent "Hey man, don't say anything. You're not out of the woods yet. Sparkie's on the way, but you're gonna make it, man." I looked down at my body, I saw tubes everywhere, and then I thought about what Tyler had just said, "Hey man, don't say anything." The thought was humorous: I couldn't say anything. I had tubes shoved down in my throat. Nonetheless, Tyler's presence brought extra comfort, and I knew if something needed to be done, he could get it done.

I glanced around at my surroundings. It was such a gloomy place. I noticed a row of cots to the left and to the right. It was dark, damp, and seemed much like a basement, and on every cot a patient lay with IVs strung above each body. The windows seemed like something one would see in a jail cell, just a small rectangular opening and a very low light shining through. The floors were bare and concrete. This to me was like no other hospital I had been in. I felt as if I were in a third–world medical facility. However, a great deal of credit and respect must be given to the doctors there. I was alive and they had done everything in their power to keep my body working. I applaud them and their willingness to work so hard to keep me, a 'foreigner,' alive. So much could be said about the healthcare in China verses the U.S., but for our purposes we will not touch on that soap-box. Moving on...

The pain in my body continued to grow. In fact, it was excruciating. I couldn't express how much pain I was in, because I couldn't speak. So, I tried through paper and pen. I wrote on a scratch pad, "Pain! Pain! PAIN!" I knew they understood because I moaned louder and louder. The nurse kept injecting my bottom, but the medicine was not working. Then, I noticed a slight change of mood in the room. Kenji and Tyler had been speaking in an intense, aggressive tone. Then, Sparkie showed up. The room turned to chaos. Sparkie was the comedian, Tyler was the tough love guy, and Kenji was the caring China-man. People and reporters were trying to get into the room. The dean and my co-teacher from the university I was teaching in even visited. Also, a few of the men who carried me out of the jungle stayed outside the hospital and wouldn't leave. The place became a zoo of high emotions.

With emotions running extremely high, I noticed an argument breaking out between Tyler and Kenji. Tyler even asked Kenji to step outside at one point, and I had no idea what the debate was over. Sometimes, in the midst of all this chaos, Tyler would look over and tell me, "Breathe man! Breathe!" My oxygen level was low, and an infection had set in on my open wound. I was headed down hill and Tyler knew it. With all the arguing and chaos in the room, I became incredibly stressed and the pain level kept rising. Finally, Tyler came over to me and said, "Hey man, just start screaming, and don't stop. Everyone's pissing me off." I didn't question what he said, I just started screaming. "Ahhhh Ahhhh Ahhhh!" Tyler said, "Louder man, and don't stop." So, louder I moaned and screamed, "AHHHH AHHHH AHHHH!" I continued screaming in pain. I saw a nurse coming my way with needle in hand, and then a sharp stick in the booty. As the meds entered, a great relief came over my body. Tyler looked down at me and said, "Better?" My facial expression said it all. Tyler exclaimed, "Brother, hang in there, I'll explain later but we got to get you out of here."

The tension increased. I had no idea what was going on but somehow plans were being made to transport me out of China. I'm still unclear of how everything worked out, but Tyler made it clear that if I stayed there, I would not recover and possibly I could die. God had brought me too far to die now. So, with pen and paper, I wrote, "Tyler, do what you think is best. I love and trust you." The truth came later and what had happened was that the doctors of Chinese medicine believe in mind over matter. I had made it through the surgery, and they were afraid of my becoming addicted to the pain medication. "What a crock of elephant poo… don't you agree reader?" Adding to this scenario, Kenji knew they were shooting me with placebos, and Tyler caught on because he knew some Mandarin. Now, in retrospect, I see what the fight was all about. It was a conflict of culture. But the right decision was made. I needed to get to a better place. The doctors there had done all they could.

I had spent four days in the China hospital. So many things circled that situation, and I will never completely know every detail. I understand that the first one contacted after my attack was Kenji. The hospital was able to reach him because of the letter he had stuck in my bag. I had planned to visit his village during my five week winter-break between semesters. He had written many phrases for me to learn, and on the same sheet of paper he wrote in Chinese, "In case of an emergency, call..." Placing his number at the bottom, he was my first point of contact. They had found my passport, camera, and one shoe in the jungle. When the hospital first called Kenji, he thought I was pranking him. Finally, after a long phone negotiation, he figured it was serious. Tyler and Kenji took the first plane out of Wuhan to Xishuangbanna. Sparkie arrived the following day. By the fourth day a plan was set in place for me to be moved to a better facility. I was leaving and I had no idea what to expect.

By this time my mom had been contacted. The local news had run the story along with other international news stations. Prayers were being lifted on my behalf world wide, from China to the U.S. and from the U.S. to Russia where my girlfriend had contacted her family about my situation. My alma mater had been notified, and even the Congresswoman Marsha Blackburn was ready to help in any way possible. I really thought a lot about my family and my sweet Ally. I wanted desperately to see her and feel her soft touch, but I knew everything was changing, and I knew I would no longer be able to do anything for her. I was certain I would be alone for the rest of my life. And that thought plagued my mind over and over.

Tyler came over to me. "Man, we have arranged for you to go to Bangkok, Thailand. Your insurance is going to fly you down there. You will be better treated and Sparkie is going with you. I can't go and they will not let Kenji in without a passport, so we are going back to Wuhan, but everything's going to work out for you man. I'm sorry you have to go through this, but you got to get out of here if you want to get any better. I think it's the best choice." I just nodded my head, and before I knew it, I was rolled out of the chamber of death and back into the world.

It was dark outside and the stroll from the hospital to the airport was a weird feeling. I met the Thai doctor in the parking lot and stated, "Doc, I don't want to feel any more pain." He said, "You don't have to worry about that. We're going to take good care of you." So, he filled me with morphine and off to the airport we headed. I was glad to be out of the basement, glad to be on the move, but in the following days and months, and actually for the next year the chamber of death concept became my own personal metaphor. I'll explain later.

## *War: POW*

Leaving China for Thailand seemed a little awkward, but that was the plan, and everyone seemed to have my best interest in mind. After being heavily drugged, they loaded me up on a large stretcher. And then, as we went through the airport, I was expecting to be airlifted via helicopter, again another 'Asian' surprise. A jumbo jet 100 passenger plane sat waiting for me and my one companion, Sparkie. They pushed my body up the ramp and onto the plane. I noticed a flight attendant open the overhead compartment and a bed folded out. I thought, "Surely, they don't expect me, a 250 pound man, to ride up there." Then suddenly, I was lifted and stuffed into place, and yes, I was bedded in the luggage compartment. As I looked around the plane, I felt as weird as I ever had. This situation was more insane than any other. A hundred passenger plane to carry me, Sparkie, the doctor, and one flight attendant seemed a little wacky. And to add to the humor of the situation, while in flight, I was turned on my left side watching Sparkie play with the stewardess. Often, he would say in a high-pitched, gallant voice, "Stewardess, stewardess." all the while holding his hand out to receive his next treat. He once looked at me and asked, "Hey doll, how does it feel to have your own personal stewardess?" I don't remember my response, but this was the most unusual flight of my life. Eventually, we landed in Bangkok, and immediately

I was back in surgery.

The hospital was modern. It seemed I had a doctor for every part of my body. Upon first arriving we went strait into surgery. The first thing they did was clean the infection that had sat in, while in the China hospital. They stabilized my body and replaced the old tubing with new tubing. The Thai nurses were so cute, and the people of Thailand amazingly friendly. The day after I arrived, a young Thai man and his girlfriend entered my room both smiling big, beautiful, loving smiles. The small Thai fellow looked at me with a look of genuine love and with a gentle, soft voice said, "Hello, my name is Aka. I am your brother." Then, the lady took the blanket off my legs and without a word she just began massaging me. Aka looked at me and said, "It is okay she do the massage?" My response was "Oh yeah, as much as she wants to." Aka and Gawn became a big part of my recovery. Their love for me is so touching. Every day they came to visit, Gawn massaged me for hours each visit. My room became a cross cultural highway filled with travelers and people who just wanted to love and support me. My new dear friend Sparkie stayed by my side almost the entire time. In fact, I had to beg him to leave. I was not used to such a wonderful family of people.

Some Thai Christians would come in and pray over me, and as they did, my spirit was breaking. I had never loved anyone the way these people loved me. All my life I had been so selfish. Aka and Gawn even slept in the hospital floor because they didn't want to leave their brother alone. They were sincerely the type of people I wished I was. God was softening my heart. I cried for hours in the presence of his love. Even now, as I write this, I have tears and snot pouring from my face. I didn't deserve to be treated so well, and I knew it. Day after day, people continued to pour in. My friend Lucy came to be my side along with so many others. I had no idea that God's family was so large and so loving. For the most part, I thought most people were evil and placed a façade of do-gooder on their faces. I thought this because I judged people based by my own mindset.

Since, converting to the Christian faith, an overwhelming spiritual war was raging within. I was exactly the person Paul had mentioned in the scripture. I sinned knowingly, and I counted grace in every situation. I was constantly manipulating God the way I thought He should be, instead of letting him mold me into His way. From the first point of my conversion, I had placed a mask upon my face, hiding all my truths. The mask disguised internal greeds and perverted thoughts. Now, that I was broken. Now, that I was hurt and in desperate need of healing, I had no choice but to reveal all the secrets I thought God may never see. As a person, God now had a better piece of clay to work with. He could now slowly peel the mask away, and His love could deepen in my heart. God grows within us, and in return, we grow into Him. To Him, a shattered jar is better to work with. For a shattered jar can be heated, melted, fixed and filled.

Sixteen days passed in the Thai hospital, twenty days from the initial attack. Up to this point, I had been treated like a celebrity. Cards, flowers, phone calls were constantly coming in. As I began reading my emails, I saw a note from Ally. It read, "Jeremy, don't die, please don't die, I need you." My heart was broken, my soul mending. Ally had been one of my best friends. She was my fleshly desire and I'm afraid she sacrificed more than me in our relationship. Now, I was sure I couldn't stay with her. I would be nothing more than dead weight, and to burden her would not be love.

The days spent in the Bangkok hospital convicted me of many things. For so long, I did not believe in miracles. For the past few years, I took what certain traditionalists had taught me and let their convictions be my regulations. I respected their knowledge of God and His word. I don't think any of them have any ill intentions, but since I walked through the valley of death, my faith changed. I can honestly claim that God miraculously intervened in my life. When I think about my intestines bulging out of my body and the blood that poured from my body for more than three hours, I can't say miracles don't happen. In fact, I live to tell people, miracles do happen. I am living proof. God does as He wills, and He willed me to live another day, and for that, I am thankful.

To make the miraculous recovery even more real, day twenty after the attack changed me even more. The doctor had come in to check on me. Sparkie, being more observant than I, asked, "Hey doc, when will he be able to walk again?" It was a question I dared not ask. The doctor replied, "Whenever he is ready." ... Miracles?

Twenty days after the four elephants attacked me, crushing nine ribs, collapsing both my lungs, puncturing my stomach, bruising my heart, breaking my shoulder and my lower back, (no one knew my shoulder and back had been broken: that was not diagnosed until months later). I began walking again. Jesus showed me so much in that moment. In my own metaphorical way, I was able to walk on water, with 'the' Christ holding my hand. "How great is our God?!"

Within a few days, I was up and about the halls of the hospital. A discharge nurse came in and said I may be discharged soon and that I would need immediate follow up when arriving back in the states. I was truly happy. Yet, it was a bitter-sweet happiness. I was going to have to leave without finishing what I set out to do. I was happy because I could see my sweet Ally. I was sad because my students may feel abandoned. I was happy because for the first time in life, I had truly missed my mom, and I desperately wanted to hug her. I was sad because I knew I may never see Kenji again. I was torn between both homes. I even considered not returning to the states and toughing out the rest of my contract, but that wasn't going to happen. My time in Asia was coming to an end, and I knew that returning to the states would have challenges of its own. I was not ready to go home, but I was ready to leave the confines of that hospital.

The next day came and the nurse discharged me. Aka and Gawn's Thai fellowship would take me in and put me up until arrangements could be made to get me back to the states. I did not hesitate to jump out of the bed after hearing this great news. As the discharge papers were handed to me, a business dressed woman entered the room. I was quick to hop out of the hospital gown and start putting normal clothing on, but before I could pull my pants up, she asked, "Mr. McGill, who will be paying the remainder of the bill your insurance didn't cover?" Not thinking much of it, I said, "I guess me. Why how much is it?" Her reply caught me off guard, "400,000 baht." My stomach turned, "Okay, lady, let's talk U.S. dollars." "About 12,000" she stated. I looked at her as I buttoned my pants. "Okay, then, I need to go to work. Just send the bill in the mail and I'll pay you when I can."

Dear reader, would you agree that by now I had been through enough? I would guess you would say "yes." Nevertheless, as if I had not already been through enough chaos, what was done next just sickened me. "Well, Mr. McGill, we can't let you leave until this bill is paid in full." Slow to anger was not my reaction. I continued to get dressed and said, "You wanna bet!" Aggressively, I gathered my belongings, as Sparkie watched on and defended me with a passive voice stating, "We told you days ago the insurance was going to run out, and you said that everything was okay." I looked to Sparkie and said, "We're leaving, come on." As I headed for the door, two guards simultaneously entered the room. I was stopped. I looked down at my body and considered busting through them, but as I thought more on this, maybe a physical struggle was the last thing I needed. I angrily turned toward the bed and stripped right back out of my clothes. "More morphine!" I shouted. Into the bed I plumped. Staring at the ceiling, I was livid. "What now? I am a prisoner. Will this war ever end?"

## *War: The Battle for Freedom*

Now, in Thai custody my temper roared. Crazy thoughts of breaking windows and kicking doors in whooshed through my mind. I was stuck and had no way out, no way of coming up with 12,000 dollars to buy my freedom. Adding intensity to the situation, the hospital would not transfer me to a cheaper room, and every day my bill would increase another 500 dollars. Sparkie, seeing my frustration, tried to calm me. He said in a gentle, loving, concerned voice, "Doll, do you really think God brought you this far to be stuck here in this hospital?" My reply, not so sweet and passive, "Sparkie, I never know what the hell God's going to do." I thought about the apostle Paul: he was a prisoner. So, maybe I was doomed to be a prisoner in a Bangkok hospital. One really never knows. As the day progressed, Sparkie sent out emails on my behalf. The world, it seemed, was in prayer. And again, I was being selfish. I doubted anyone would come to my rescue. After all I had been through, I still had doubt. I guess the humanity never ceases, even after walking on water.

Many visitors came in and out of my new 'cell.' I remember one person saying, "Don't worry, you're on the Christian hotline. We'll get you out of here." But that didn't settle well. "Why would anyone want to help me?" I thought. "Doesn't everyone have enough of their own problems to worry about?" Behind the scenes, however, a mass of people began working together for my freedom and return to the U.S.

The following few days, I tried escaping and finding the humor in the situation. More and more people would come and visit. I started sharing the story more openly, even with people I didn't know. I took for granted what God had already brought me through and began to let his power work through me. I was sharing God's love with a variety of people. One man, a middle-eastern Muslim, comes to mind in particular. Before the elephant attack, I may have viewed this man as a sort of enemy. But now that my heart was softened, I see him only as a man. I see him as a child of God, a child of God on a journey, a spiritual journey just like me. We shared our thoughts on God and pretty much both came to the same conclusion. God does work miracles. Though we both had a different name for God, we at least had one common thread, and that was that something bigger than ourselves was at work in our lives, and truly it was no coincidence that we met.

Keeping the humor of the situation was sometimes difficult. Walking out through the hospital halls, being followed and radio monitored was somewhat discomforting. Then, I let loose and decided to have a little fun. Sparkie and I entered an elevator. One guard radioed the other guard. One guard stepped onto the elevator with us, trying to pretend he wasn't following us. As Sparkie and I made passing comments, we decided to have a little fun with this guy. I commented that he wasn't doing a good job, secretly following me. He said nothing. I decided to take the situation to the next level. I grabbed the guard, took his arm, and placed it around my head. It appeared that he had me in a headlock; he must have been terribly confused. Sparkie began laughing and taking pictures of the whole thing. The guard eventually saw our humor and laughed along with us. As the saying goes, when life hands you lemons, make lemonade. I had truly had a few of life's lemons handed to me over the past few weeks, and it was time for some refreshing lemonade. Laughter truly is one of the greatest remedies, that and morphine.

As the hours of my imprisonment passed by ever so slowly, I was forming a true bond with Sparkie. We continued to raise cane and mess with the hospital guards. A meeting was soon set up with the lady who seemed to have control over my freedom. Sparkie, knowing my personality, asked that I let him deal with negotiations. I wasn't having it. It was my freedom. Sparkie made me promise I wouldn't get mad and that I would be Christian during the meeting. My reply, "Sparkie, I will be nice." I don't know what came over me, but as I sat in the small, office cubical in my hospital gown, a great anger arose within. This lady had the key to my freedom, and I couldn't stand it. As soon as she came around the corner, I couldn't contain myself. The next thing I knew I was throwing stuff at her and wasn't turning the other cheek. I realized I had let Sparkie down, and I just took off. As I angrily made my way through the hospital halls, I looked back and noticed there were no guards. "Aha!" I could escape.

I made my way down to the lobby. I noticed people were looking at me, but they weren't guarding me. I then slipped out the exit door and found myself hidden from the guards across the way by some sort of delivery van. It was a narrow street, and if I could just stay behind the van and wait for the right traffic situation, I could indeed escape. The perfect situation presented itself. The van slowly began moving toward the main roadway. It moved at such a pace that I could crouch behind it and walk at the same speed. As the van shielded my body, we crept down the alley. Eventually, the driver sped away, and I took off walking as fast as I could. Injured and out of breath, I made my way to freedom. There at the end of the alley, I looked down at my feet, I had no shoes. I stood in a hospital gown baring much of my body in the wind. I looked right and noticed a man looking at me with a confused expression. "What now?" I asked myself. I didn't know where to go. I really didn't even know where I was. This was the first time I had left the hospital. It was the first time I had been outside on my own two feet in nearly a month. Even if I knew where I wanted to go, I had no money to get there. I looked up and felt the sunshine on my face. It was that freedom I needed most, and through my own twisted way, it was enough to satisfy me. I knew my best choice would be to return to the confines of the hospital.

I made my way back to the hospital. Looking at the guards, I smiled. As I passed them by, I said, "No worries, I'm going back to my room." I made my way back through the hospital and entered my room where Sparkie was waiting. I apologized to him for my conduct and gently laid my broken body back in the bed. It was comfortable, and I was better off there than anywhere else. Sometimes our prisons can be our best homes. We just don't know it until we've escaped. Meanwhile, while I was plotting and scheming others were hard at work on my behalf. Plans were being made to free me and get me back to the states. I don't know the whole story, but what I do know I will share.

Channel Four News out of Nashville, Tennessee, ran the story. A medical fund was set up through some Christians in Spanish Fort, Alabama. That medical fund was then transferred to my old college, Freed-Hardeman University. As the world watched on through the news and through the internet, prayers were being lifted, and funds were being transferred. Within four days, three times the money needed was raised for my release. God's children once again conquered my heart with their love. I was amazed at how many people truly cared, especially those who never even met me. Cards poured in, emails filled my inbox, my facebook wall and myspace page overflowing with loving, kind, and encouraging words. A great warm fuzzy feeling surrounds my body just thinking back on that day. God's love was being poured out on me, and I was overwhelmed with awe. In the midst of this spiritual arousal, Neal entered the room. Neal was an English teacher in Thailand. He and his wife had come to visit me almost daily. He said, "Hey brother, got something to show you."

Neal turned his laptop on, and set it on my lap, and

faced it toward me. Through the screen, the Nashville news station reported:

"A Mount Juliet man is recovering in Thailan after he was attacked by an elephant in China. Nancy McGill said her son, Jeremy, is Mr. Adventure. He has been skydiving, written a book about his hike across America, and since August, has been in central China teaching English.

But McGill said he's best known for his humor, so when she got a call Friday from his friend in China saying that Jeremy had been attacked by a wild elephant, she was sure it was a joke.

"I sat on the phone waiting for the punch line to come and (hear) him maybe on three-way and laughing saying, 'Gotcha,'" said McGill.

But the joke never came.

After the attack, her 30-year-old son from Mount Juliet was left unconscious and in critical condition after an elephant picked him up by its trunk and threw him in the air.

"He was going to die, that's what first went through my mind," said McGill.

The attack happened as Jeremy McGill was touring Wild Elephant Valley, a nature reserve in the Yunnan Province of China.

"Both his lungs were punctured. His stomach was punctured. His ribs were broken, and his left shoulder was broken," said McGill.

It's unclear why the elephant snapped but Jeremy was reportedly taking a picture of the animals when another attacked him.

The bizarre attack made the news nationally in China.

Jeremy McGill was transported to Thailand under the care of special doctors and is listed in serious condition.

McGill spoke with her son on Sunday night for the first time after the attack.

"Last night I could understand the words he was saying, so he is better, much better. Yes, he is going to make it," said McGill.

A spokesman for Chinese Foreign Affairs said elephants have attacked tourists at that reserve before.

He said in the previous attacks, the elephants were spooked by camera flashes or loud noises, but it was unclear on Monday was caused this recent incident.

A fund has been set up for McGill.

Freed-Hardeman University in Henderson, Tenn., is accepting donations for the Jeremy McGill Medical Fund."

When the news report finished, I was in tears, I missed my mom, and I wanted desperately to hug her. Seeing her on the news, I felt her sadness. I felt my mom's spirit crying out for her son. I've always had a good connection with my mother but everything a mom and son have, came together all at once, in that moment. I was her baby, and she loved me the best she knew how. Our bond at that moment was stronger than ever before, and I wanted to comfort her. I was ready to go home. The next day funds were transferred to the Bangkok International Hospital. I was released and taken in by the Thai church.

It would be a few days before arrangements to fly

me out could be made. Sunday morning came and I was asked to speak. The Thai preacher translated. As I told the story, I felt the spirit moving within me, and I knew my life was forever changed. I had walked into and through the valley of death. I came out, a new man with a spirit of fear and love. God's power to save me was transforming me from the inside out. I had so many questions; I had so many doubts, and the battle had just begun.

## *War: And...A War Within*

After being released from the hospital I hung out with Aka, Gawn, and the Thai church. Sparkie and I were touring the city and being treated like VIP's. We had escorts everywhere. I loved the Thai experience but time had come for me to make my trek back to America. My initial reaction was to go back to China and complete my teaching contract. But really, I knew that wasn't physically possible. However, I was not going to leave without saying good-bye to Kenji and my Chinese Christian family and some of the students. So, my first flight was back to Wuhan. I was warmly welcomed by Kenji and my co-teacher Allen.

Arriving back in Wuhan, I was surrounded daily by friends and my Chinese family. I desperately wanted to stay, but decisions and provisions for my health had been made. I went along with what others suggested. I was in a great deal of pain. I wanted so much to stay, but at the same time I was ready to go back home, see my mom, and hold Ally in my arms. As my mind played forward into my future, I saw my mom and friends waiting on me at the airport. There among them would be precious Ally. I wanted so bad just to be alone with her. I wanted to hold her and have her hold me. If at that moment I had one wish it would be to be alone in a dark room with the lady I had planned to propose to. A woman's touch always seems to make the pain disappear.

Once at the Wuhan airport, I was preparing my heart for departure. I was shuffled about between Kenji, Wing, and Allen. I was strolled through the airport in a wheelchair. My China adventure had come to an end. The experience was more than I ever expected, now the hard part, saying good-bye, especially, saying good bye to Kenji. We hugged repeatedly before being forced through the airport's checking station. As we were separated by the airport gates, I looked back and saw Kenji. Tears strolling down both our cheeks, we had to both be wondering the same thing, "Will I ever get to see him again?" I lifted my arm to say good-bye. He was the best friend a man could ever ask for. By my side he came and in my heart he will always remain. Then, as I turned my back, another battle ensued and the war within begin to tear at my spirit.

"Dear Kenji, I know not if I will ever see you on this earth again. I only know that we are true brothers. I miss you so much. My life has forever changed because of you and your love for God and for me. I don't know if this letter will ever find its way to you, but I do know we will surely unite again in heaven. Kenji, I still carry those tears with me from the day we had to say good-bye. I'm doing everything I know how to get back to you. Like a message in a bottle, thrown into the ocean, I hope one day this letter finds you. Remember brother, we are only a prayer away." Always yours, Jeremy.

As I boarded the plane, I sighed with uncertainty. The trip to China began playing over and over in my head. I remembered the first day to the last one: The Great Wall climb with Adam, the midnight mountain climb with my student Michael, the time Kenji and I went fishing and chaos broke out, the time that I wore a mask and scared the locals, the Chinese Christmas party, my 30$^{th}$ birthday party, my students, my first class, New Years with Kenji and Lucy, karaoke, the food, the sounds, the smiles, the love, and then the elephants. Was I making the right choice? Should I have stayed longer? I was being flown first class to L.A. and many people I loved were awaiting my arrival. I sat back in the comfort of first class, said a few words to the guy beside me, took my pain meds, and dozed off.

"Okay, passengers, please sit up and fasten your seatbelts. We will soon be landing at LAX. The time is now…. The weather…" I was now arriving back home, but nothing felt right. I was at an awkward crossroads in life. I had so many things to figure out. So many doubts filled my mind and so many questions still unanswered. What would I do with my life? The truths that many people search for were now answered through a crazy episode with four elephants. I was torn apart on the inside. And had no idea what choices I would make next. I just knew I wanted the medicine to never run out, and I wanted to be held by my lady. I wanted the world to disappear, and I felt the need to crawl in a cave and hide away. Yet, I was put in the spotlight and wheeled through the airport. "Welcome back to the U.S. Mr. McGill." said the customs clerk. I felt a sense of accomplishment and failure all at one time. My flight to Nashville would not come until the next morning. It seemed a never ending transition.

I stayed at a close by hotel and ordered a Papa John's pizza. As I looked out my hotel window, I thought a lot about the differences of my country and China. Staring out at the LA lights, I thought: Life is truly interesting, our world is full of life, people come and people go, but no matter when and how, we all certainly go. We all live and we all die. And life, it really is a journey that shouldn't be taken for granted. It is over in the blink of an eye. As I thought back on the past few months, I realized one path led to another, and each path has its' own consequences. Heaven or hell is not the issue. The path we choose, the way we love, the people we share our hearts with, those are the things to be focused on. Yes, there is a heaven and hell, and Christ is the way to heaven, for He has told us, "I AM THE WAY." And at the same time, so are the people we encounter. The way we treat them, the way we place their lives above our own, that's what's going to echo in eternity. Knowing this truth, knowing how truly fragile life can be caused a storm to brew deep inside my soul. I questioned myself, "Do I have the courage to lose it all? Am I strong enough to let God take control?" This war is within us all.

The next day I flew into the Nashville airport. A man with a wheelchair waited for me on the ramp. As he gathered my bags and began pushing me through the airport, he began explaining that there were news people waiting out in the lobby. I said, "Yeah man, they are waiting on me." He replied, "Really?" I said, "It's a long story man." He simply said, "Okay" and pushed me into the lobby.

As I was wheeled into the waiting area, there stood my mother. She ran to me. Tears in her eyes, she pleaded, "My baby! My baby!" and hugged me with pride. I looked around and there was my brother and sister and their loved ones. There were unexpected friends and my best pal, Richard Petty. I had not so long ago seen them all at my funeral. Now, I was seeing them in the afterlife. It is still an odd time to recollect. But the one thing I noticed most was that Ally was not there. I knew she was busy with her schooling, but I thought possibly she might surprise me. I guess we all have different perspectives on what is the responsible and right thing to do. I think this might have been the moment I seriously questioned my relationship with her. The war within brewed stronger and stronger.

At mom's house was a warm welcoming home party. I was glad to see so many of my friends. It still awed me that these same people were just a month ago attending my funeral. I was at home, but I was not at peace. After two days of seeing my hometown friends and family of Mount Juliet, it was now time to go and meet Ally. Mom and Dad drove me into West Tennessee. We picked up the young Russian princess and she was as adorable as before. However, she was a little reluctant to hold me. We spent the night in a hotel room trying to get reacquainted with each other. I had all these dreams of marrying this woman, but now I wasn't sure. I was different and I knew it. She was the same great person she had always been, but our dreams were different. I had walked on water, and a month later she was baptized, but things were not lining up for us.

Ally is by far one of the most perfect women I have ever encountered. Any man would be blessed to have her as a wife. She is truly a precious part of my heart. I know this for sure. Her heart is golden. We spent a lot of time together, spring came and went, and then so did summer. I was still in a tremendous amount of pain. I had followed her to Nashville because that was where she landed a teaching job. I on the other hand, had not yet landed any job and was still uncertain about what I should do. I hated living in Nashville. I wanted something more. I was being flown all over the U.S. and was being paid to give my testimony. It seemed everyone wanted to hear the elephant story, even some people out in Hollywood. They even made two shows about my life, but still there was emptiness, and the pain pills were becoming more of a crutch.

My 31st birthday soon came. Fall had set in and the leaves were changing. Life was being lived, and I was dying on the inside. I watched my surroundings and saw that people were moving forward, and I had come to a stale phase in life with no desire to do anything, but lay in a cloud of narcotics. I hated my life and needed desperately to find my purpose again. I asked Ally if she would come camping with me for my birthday. Her response was a classic Ally question. "What will we do there?" It hit me then, she was not the one for me. I desperately wanted her to be the one, but I knew our personalities were clashing. I liked roughing it, and Ally was a city girl. She enjoyed the comforts of life, and who was I to ask her to be something she wasn't? We just weren't compatible.

Ally came camping with me. She sacrificed her comforts for my happiness, and we had a good time, but deep within me I knew I had a choice to make. Would I sacrifice my comforts and ask this lady to be my bride? Would I settle for a white, picket fence and the American dream? Or, would I break things off and be alone in the world and pray God send me an angel of mercy? October 12, 2008, was the most miserable birthday ever. I decided our romance was to end. Never in all my life had I broken off a friendship with anyone. Ally had been one of my best friends for the past two years. I loved her, I really loved her, but I knew she was not the right one for me, and I was definitely not the right one for her.

Late that afternoon on a canoe in the middle of a peaceful stream we had our last fight. The result of our argument left us holding each other crying all night in our tent. My eyes soaked her shirt and our pillows with tears of great sorrow. Her tears gave me even more sorrow. I felt so bad for having to hurt her, it was never my intention, but it was the right choice, a very hard choice, but the right choice. I had to let her go, if I truly loved her, I would set her free for the right guy to come along and love her the way she deserved to be loved and the way she wanted to be loved. I simply wasn't that guy. The storm had come; the sea had swallowed my heart. A war was fought, no victor announced. Yet, the battle continued. Ally went her way and I? Well, I entered a lonely, dark, desperate place. I didn't feel alive anymore. I was completely dead on the inside. I call this part of my life the dungeon of depression.

## *War: Dungeon of Depression*

Songs of sorrow, whiskey, and pills filled the days and nights of my life. I was deep in darkness. If you stepped into my life, you would have seen a fat sack of bones, a man with many sorrows, and a man with no hope. I had every excuse to be depressed. Over the past four to five years, I had fought drug addictions. Now, all I had to do was see the doctor and I could get whatever I wanted. I was thirty-one with two college degrees, living in my grandmother's basement. I was somewhat disabled from the elephant attack and now just taking a walk or even driving seemed to add to the misery. I had buried my daughter ten years ago, and many believed I never dealt with that pain. Again, her death was revisited by my loneliness. I was now without hope of ever finding true love. I guess that hurt the worse. The thought of going through life without a partner was just too much for my heart to take. There were options though, I could end it all. I could take that black, shiny gun; place it in my mouth, and BOOM! No more struggles. Or, I could, for my family's sake, crash the car into a tree or pole and no-one would have to know I took the easy way out. Or, I could simply just disappear. I could pack up a small bag and live in the streets, give up on life, and just be a bum. All these options seemed better than what I was actually doing, which was nothing more than becoming another welfare case. "Oh pity me, life has treated me horrible, don't I deserve a little rest. It just isn't fair."

If by chance one were to visit me, he would have seen a full grown slob. As the winter months rolled in, I nailed blankets over the windows. I slept all day and worked just enough to pay for my gas and to get my drugs. I was back to what I had left years ago. I was living in a dark, damp basement. I was taking my medicine and using them intravenously. A spoon, some water, and little pills became my best friends. I was the same person I tried so hard not to be. After all the trials of life, I ended right back where I started twelve years prior, doping up in a parents basement, not caring about the outside world, only doing what could fill my flesh and my emptiness. Maybe this was who I truly was and I couldn't escape my past. Maybe, I was nothing more than a drug-addicted, substance-abusing addict. Maybe, God didn't save my soul from hell; instead, I was doomed to repeat another life of misery. Many thoughts of death filled my days. How I made it through could be nothing more than divine intervention.

Christmas approached and I tried to have some joy. I even threw a Christmas party in the basement. I was miserable, but every year I had a Christmas bash. Though I was depressed, I still wanted to see the people I loved. Many came to the party, and from what I hear, it was an alright gig. I slept most of the time, for in my sleep, I had no reality.

Next, a new year was born. I simply tried to let go of the pain by stepping into a dark bar of lonely souls, and even there I saw people happier than I. So, when it was time to toast 2009, I raised my glass of champagne and with all the others toasting a new beginning, I lifted my glass to another day of dark misery. There was no feeling of newness. My life was ruined, I felt dead. All I really wanted was to be left alone to my pills and my dungeon of depression. And for the next several months that's exactly what I did. I sat in darkness as Satan continually whispered in my ear.

It was the longest winter of my life. In fact, it had been the longest year of my life. In January of 2008, I thought I had it all figured out. I was a college professor traveling the world. I had a beautiful girl friend whom I would soon marry. I had two college degrees and was ready to pursue a PhD. I had written one book and had many other adventures to write about. I was what I thought the world may envy. Then, on that fateful day, those four wild elephants had to go and mess everything up. They broke me up really bad. I was sure death was upon me. Lying there on the jungle floor, I was satisfied with the life I had lived, or at least, I thought I was satisfied. Maybe it's more appropriate to state that I was satisfied with what people would think about, when they thought about the life of Jeremy McGill. I realized I had led a full life, yet truly, in my own personal way, my life had never been fulfilled.

It was now January 2009, and all those dreams I had just a year ago were nothing more than an illusion. I was certain my destiny was loneliness. I had once been the center of the world, or so I thought. But now, I was fading away and soon I would be forgotten. To quicken the process, I began pushing everyone away. I even treated my mother and grandmother like crap. They had done nothing to deserve my pain. I ignored my friends and continued to block other relatives out of my life. I wanted nothing to do with them. Their happiness meant nothing to me. My happiness was gone, and I wanted the world to end. As I watched the stock market crashing and a recession setting in, I thought, "That's right! That's what we all deserve. Greedy American bastards, how dare you live life without me? I hate you all." My spirit was now filled with anger. No longer was I just depressed, I was pissed, and selfishly, I wanted the rest of civilization to sink with me. I saw my life as a hollow jar of misery. How can anyone be happy? In fact, what is happiness? Isn't happiness just a fake emotion that will soon crumble under God's unjust design?

Depression is a lonely place. Only those who have lived there can ever understand it. Sure, we all have our ups and downs. That's life. Sure, we get sad and angry when things don't go our way. We all have pain and we all need pain. Without pain could we ever truly appreciate happiness? I was certain that God had left me to live a life of misery and sorrow. I also knew I didn't deserve the grace He offered, so I wished He had just taken me the day the elephants attacked. And it may be that someone today is reading these words. It may be that someone is you or someone else you know of who may be in a valley of depression. I beg you now, do as my grandmother and many others did for me. Patiently love them. Never give up praying for them. If they are here alive on earth,

I promise, they still have a great purpose to fulfill.

It's amazing what desperate, depressed people will do. I was willing to do anything to escape the pain. I knew medication was not enough. I began looking for other escape routes. I was desperate for attention; I even created a fake personality. I created a profile on the internet and I named him William Ulysses Change. In short the name was a question, Will U. Change? He was going to be my social outlet.

The cliché states, "Sometimes we have to hit rock bottom before we can ever start climbing back up." I am a true believer in this. It is when we are broken and in desperate need that God can do his most mighty works. It takes a desire and an effort to conquer depression. It takes will to find purpose in the pain life gives us. Today, as I began to conclude this short story, I am the happiest, most blessed man I know. And from the dungeon of depression to the pinnacle of a mountain, I am so glad this story found its way into your hands. I can feel the spirit boiling within me. It is like I'm about to unlock a secret that may conquer the devil's strong hold on so many people's lives. This secret has to be shared. It has to be told. I am anxious and excited to reveal what the real meaning of Elephant Juice is really all about. As I laid in that dark dungeon of depression, a spark within was flamed by a divine power. This divine power lives within us all; we just need to allow the right wind to set it ablaze. I still stand amazed. I've said it once, and I'll say it a hundred times more, the juice is good.

## *The Road Home:*
## *Love from Above*

As the winter of 2009 came to an end, life began springing up all around. It was March and the days became longer. Grass was being cut, flowers were blooming, and trees were sprouting green happiness on each seemingly dead limb. In particular, I can remember the yellow flowers that seem to pop up everywhere. They had once disappeared in the deadness of winter, but, like so many of God's creations, it was time for a new bloom. I, like the flowers, had withered away it seemed, and like the rest of God's creation, I was also ready to bloom again. As the seasons change, so do our lives. I was tired of dying and too afraid to actually end my own life. I was ready for a change of seasons within myself. So, what did I do? Everything but the right thing, but I did take action however, and taking action is the first step to conquering depression.

I was out of money, out of pain meds, and I needed some kind of release. I decided to go and visit the emergency room. I thought if they just took a serious look at me, they would have some sympathy and maybe give me some kind of shot to ease my back pain. My back was broken but healing. I found this out not through a doctor but from someone who knew me and sent me the documentation through an email. The doctors had misdiagnosed me at first, and did not treat me. This happened more than once and at two different hospitals. Also, my blood pressure had been high every time because of the pain I had to deal with and the anxiety from Post Traumatic Stress Disorder (PTSD). Nightmares plagued my dreams daily. I seemed helpless and felt that no one really wanted to help. So, I decided to try a different hospital.

Sometime after midnight, I headed downtown Nashville to the general hospital. The previous ER visits had been a failure. I was not treated as a person but rather as an unwanted problem. Even though I had fresh scars and multiple broken bones, I was never x-rayed and never taken seriously. So, this time I was going prepared. I took a bottle of forty sleeping pills with me. If the doctors didn't take me serious, I would in turn swallow the sleeping pills and force them to take me seriously. I entered the ER and was treated great at first. My blood pressure was a little high, my pain very intense, and my need for medical care desperate. The doctor came in and for thirty minutes I spilled my heart out to him. I explained I wanted to get better and that other hospitals had neglected me and tried to treat my pain with anti-inflammatory shots. He said, "Sounds like you been through a lot. Don't worry. We will take good care of you." Finally, someone seemed to care, or did he? He sent his orders to the nurse.

The nurse came through the hospital curtain, needle in hand, and with a polite tone she said, "Okay, we got a little something to ease your pain." Curiously, I said, "What is it?" Her reply, "It's an anti-inflammatory." Angered, depressed, I couldn't believe it. "I refuse to pay for that shot! I just got through explaining to the doctor that I have had that shot, and it does not work. Just get me a drink of water, please." She looked at me with discontent, "So, you're refusing the medication?" I could barely contain myself, "Please just get me a cup of water." She turned around and then came back in with a cup of water and discharge papers in her hand. She handed me the cup of water, and asked me to sign off, and I did. Then, as she turned, I took the entire bottle of prescription sleeping pills, and with the cup of water, I swallowed all forty pills. I immediately walked through the ER and found the doctor sitting behind a desk, with his feet propped up, reading a magazine. I looked him square in the eyes, slammed the empty prescription bottle down, and said, "I just took this whole bottle, maybe now you will take me serious!" I went back to my little waiting area, what happened next was the last thing I ever expected to happen.

Lying on the tiny, hard bed, waiting for some kind of relief, two security officers with the doctor entered the room. I was asked to leave the premises. I couldn't believe it. I had obviously just overdosed in an act of desperation, and instead of treating me the doctor had me removed. I could have died. He didn't care. Now, I was scared. I hurried to the closest other ER. I did not hesitate to find a nurse and tell her what I had just done. She asked, "Why would you do that?" I simply said, "I need help, and no-one seems to listen." She wasted no time. She rushed me back to the ER and within moments I had some relief. I was glad that someone cared. I finally got a few hours of sleep and a little pain relief.

Nevertheless, my desperate action came with unattended consequences.

The next morning came, and I was awakened by two police officers. They handcuffed me and took me to the nut house. I knew my choice was a bad one, but I never expected to be imprisoned. They admitted me as a suicidal, depressed patient. And truly I was out of my mind, but now I was embarrassed. I made a foolish, heat of the moment decision and now I was stuck. I wanted desperately to return to the dungeon of depression. At least there I had some control of my life. I felt like I was being punished for being an injured man. Yes, I knew I was depressed. I was thirty-one years old, living in my grandmother's basement. I had two college degrees and my life was going nowhere. I had just pushed all my friends and family away, including a chance at having a wife. I felt unworthy of anything, and I was certain now I would spend my last days on earth alone and in pain. I had no hope. I wanted death or I wanted to find the silver lining. One or the other needed to happen and happen quickly.

This was the second time in my life I found myself locked up in a mental institution, and I have to admit both times helped tremendously. Though it is embarrassing, I am glad there are such institutions. I wish everyone had the privilege to experience such a place just for one week. I know that it would do everyone some good. And trust me, you never want to start a conversation out with a psychiatrist like I did. Once they got me into the institution, I explained, "I know this sounds crazy, but I really was attacked by wild elephants in China." The doctor next asked if I was hearing voices and seeing things. My response, "Yes! I see you, and I hear all kinds of things." He asked next, "Are you depressed?" Answer: "Duh? Of course I am depressed. I am in constant pain and my life has fallen apart! You don't need a degree to figure that out." After this episode, I refused all treatment. I felt like I was unjustly imprisoned, but as I prayed upon the situation, I saw the silver lining. I did have hope. I was not dead yet, and now I was at a perfect place to clear my head and get in a few laughs.

The patients there were truly a delight to be with. When it seemed that no one else cared for me, those people dealing with their own demons helped me in ways no counselor, no friend, no family, and no other specialist could. I saw within them that I was wasting my life, my gift, and now I had a choice to redeem myself. And so, with humility I reached out. Within a few days, I was released back into society. I went back to my dungeon of depression, but I was ready to take the blankets off the windows. Spring had come in perfect harmony with the seasonal change within my soul. All I needed now was a push and some inspiration.

Days went by and I was searching. I felt a little fire within begin to burn. I needed an adventure, something that would bring Jeremy McGill back to life, living life to the fullest, as I had always done before. I began searching for inspirational videos on the internet. I have always been inspired by films and music. I just needed the right movie and the right song to get me motivated.

I remember coming across a YouTube *Gladiator* video. The music was that of Metallica and the song *Hero of the Day*. Then, I watched "Into the Wild," a story about a man who went out searching for happiness in the lone wilderness of Alaska. In the end, he shared that true happiness was shared with people. So, the plan to canoe the Mississippi river alone didn't seem right, but I needed an adventure, and I needed it soon. I couldn't sleep. Many thoughts of just disappearing kept coming through my mind. To leave life and become a mystery always seemed appealing, but it just wasn't the right thing. It would be a selfish journey, so what could I do? Then, some divine intervention, everything came together and my life was about to drastically make another change.

Sometime around 4am I was watching Christian network television. A man named Joseph Prince was preaching. His message was right on. It was as if he was speaking directly to me. He spoke about the power of God being within us and how God reigns in the world and that darkness has no chance of overcoming our light. I got that warm fuzzy feeling we all like, and I sat in tears, because I knew he was speaking the truth. God loved me, and He had kept me alive through so many horrid experiences, including being attacked by four wild elephants. I knew God had a purpose for me; I just had been suppressing it with my selfish pity. Then, later in the same day a news commentator for Fox News came on. Glenn Beck was educating Americans through his opinions and researched facts, but one thing stuck out the most. Glenn, in short, was telling Americans to get off their butts and get busy. He stated that success comes from hard work and dedication, and I knew I needed to be doing both. After being lifted by Glenn's passion, I looked through my movies. I found a DVD I had purchased in China and remembered it was quite inspiring. The last time I had watched it was with Kenji, so I popped in Rocky Balboa, and for as long as I may live, I can honestly say this movie changed my life forever. Let me set it up for you:

So, Rocky is old and retired now. His son has grown up, his wife Adrianne has passed on, and he is just kind of drifting through life. But there is something deep within him, something he referred to as the basement. He said he had a lot of stuff pinned up and he just wanted to release it. There was a lion so-to-speak inside him. All Rocky's life he had been a fighter, and he had yet to make his grand exit. He needed one more fight; he needed to get the stuff out of the basement, so he could reach that peace we all look for in life. He knew the only way to calm the lion was to release it. Rocky was ready to fight again, because for no other reason than that was just who he was, a fighter. But like so many people in life, everyone seemed to think he was crazy. "Man you're too old." "Rocky, what do you have to prove?" "You don't have a chance, give it a rest." He applied for a boxing license, and though he passed the batteries of physical test required for a license, the judges had already made a decision. Although he passed the physical examinations with flying colors, the court ruled against licensing Rocky to box. Rocky, not being one to ever back down, fought back with what Americans need to hear, the pursuit of happiness. It is our right, and we should never allow anything or anybody to stand in our way, but then came the punch line.

Of all the people Rocky wanted to be by his side and support him the most, it had to be his son. But like the rest of the nay-sayers, his son thought he was crazy. Disappointed in his own life, he blamed his father for his own failures. He claimed Rocky had cast too big of a shadow for him to ever have a life of his own. And now, with Rocky entering the ring again, he could not see anything but the negative. He was the depressed son. Rocky's son, like me, had all these excuses that held him down, and Rocky came back with the greatest quote of all time, and it fit perfectly in my life. It was like God had talked to me through a screen play written by Sylvester Stallone, and the quote goes like this:

*"Let me tell you something you already know. The world ain't all sunshine and rainbows. It is a very mean and nasty place and I don't care how tough you are, it will beat you to your knees and keep you there permanently if you let it. You, me, or nobody is gonna hit as hard as life.* ***But it ain't about how hard you hit; it's about how hard you can get hit, and keep moving forward.*** *It's How much you can take, and keep moving forward. That's how winning is done. Now, if you know what you're worth, then go out and get what you're worth. But you gotta be willing to take the hits, and not point fingers and blame other people. Cowards do that and that ain't you. You're better than that!"*

Life sure had beaten me down. I buried my first born at eight months old. My wife of three years had abandoned me for no good reason at all. I had overdosed on drugs several times. At age twenty-two, my colon was perforated, and I had an emergency surgery to save my life, which left me having to live with a colostomy bag. I had been run over by 2 cars and can't number the wrecks I had been in. I had fallen off fifty foot cliffs and broken several bones. I had been homeless, found lying in ditches, drunken and beaten. I had been mugged and beaten to a point where I was blind for nearly a week. When I played football, my bone popped out my right leg. I had so many faults; I had lived my youth as an outlaw, my skull cracked, my love life destroyed by so many fleshly desires. And then just when I thought I was going to get to the top, those damn elephants attacked me, and we all know how busted up I was after that. Pain, that motto belonged to me. Now, I was living alone depressed, and life had hit just about as hard as it could, but those words from Rocky echoed into my spirit: *"it ain't about how hard you hit; it's about how hard you can get hit, and keep moving forward. It's how much you can take, and keep moving forward. That's how winning is done."*

I was beaten, but I wasn't dead, and I sure wanted to be a winner. No longer did I want to sit in pity. Rocky's quote spoke straight to my heart. I stood with both hands raised in the air and decided it was time to come alive again. I was done dying and was ready to start living. I ran up the steps and exclaimed loudly to my granny, "I'm leaving!" She looked disturbed and said, "Leaving where?" I was alive, my spirit had awakened, and all I knew to say was, "Granny, I love you, I don't know where I'm going or where I will live, but anywhere is better than this dungeon of depression."

I walked downstairs, took the blankets off the windows, and finished watching *Rocky Balboa*. In the end, Rocky didn't win the fight, but he won the battle. He had been beaten all his life, but he wasn't backing down, and now, I was ready to stand back up on my own two feet. I was ready to change my destiny. I knew it was going to be a tough road back to normalcy. For the past year, I had done nothing but become a welfare bum, and pitied myself. Now, renewed with the love from above, I was ready to step back out into the light. I didn't know where or how, but I was about to take some sort of action. I was determined to regain what Satan had tried to take away. For a moment the wicked one had stolen my hope and faith; I had gone through a dark valley and God was not only bringing me through the valley, but he was about to place me on the summit of life's mountain. My dear friends, I cannot express to you how crazy this journey turns out. All I can say is keep sipping the elephant juice. It will satisfy your thirst.

## *The Road Home: Hope*

A canoe ride down the mighty Mississippi was my first thought. If I could just go and be a part of nature, maybe that would blaze the spark that had occurred within. I looked at what it would take to canoe from Tennessee to the Gulf of Mexico. Yet, there was still a loneliness about that. I needed people. I am by nature a very socialistic person. Where could I go? What could I do? I needed work, I needed money, and I needed physical rehabilitation. I needed to toughen up. My back was hurt, my shoulder still busted, but I still had some parts that were able to do something, and then it hit me, physical labor. Of all the people in my life, only a few do I remember calling me while I was depressed, my good friend Bethany Odom, Judy Prince, Richard Petty, and Mike Harris. And so, I gave it a gamble. I called Mike.

"Hey man, I just want you to know, I really appreciate you calling and checking in on me. I've been down in the dumps, man. My back hurts constantly, and I only got one good arm. I'm calling you for two reasons, one to say thanks and another, because I need work. I need hard physical labor to strengthen myself and get out of this rut." Mike's reply, "Well, come on. I got all the back breaking work you can handle." Mike is the owner of Logan's Lake aperies. It's a bee farm, but he does a lot of other farming as well. It's hard, hot work and I had before been his right hand man. I knew if I was going to work with him again, it was going to hurt like hell, but it may be just the right thing to do. So against most logic, I headed out.

I packed my car, a tent, a sleeping bag, a few fishing poles, and some old clothes. The next day I told my grandmother bye. Worried sick, she asked, "Where will you stay?" My reply was very disturbing to her, "Granny, I've got nothing to lose, but everything to gain. I'm going to live in the woods. I'm going to work my way back up to what ever it is God has for me to do. I know it seems crazy and irrational, but I got to do this." And like so many other times before, she hugged me and said, "Jeremy, I love you, but remember Jesus loves you more." I tried to comfort her with words like, "Don't worry, I'm going to get back on top where I belong. I just need to go."

As I packed my belongings, I began thinking back on all I had lost. I began thinking about how I went from a professor in China to a bum in Nashville. I had pushed so many people away. I decided before I left, I would give one final call to one of those I probably hurt the most, Ally. When I called, she answered the phone. She was very busy, but decided to meet me. We met by the lake, and I apologized to her for being such a jerk. We held hands by the water's edge, and I spilt a little of my heart, "Ally, I've been through hell, you know that. I've pushed everyone away, and I feel I don't have any friends left, but I want you to know one thing, I do care about you. I'm all messed up inside, but I promise you this one thing, the next time you see me, Jeremy McGill will be back on top of the world." She looked at me with a genuine tear forming in her eye, and said, "I know you will Jeremy, I feel it. It's like a rock; you have many great things to do. God kept you alive for some reason, so go and get back to your old self." We hugged for a few seconds, and kissed on the cheek. I got in my vehicle, looking back at the lady I used to think would be my future wife. As I drove off into the sunset headed west, tears of pain and joy rolled down my cheeks. I knew Ally wasn't the one. She had always been a good friend. I only wish the best for her; she deserves it. However, there was one thing I did not reveal; there was no way for me to become my old self. I had died, and I had come back to life, a new life. It was scary in its own way, but I had two choices, die or face my fears.

I left Nashville headed down Interstate Forty West. I wasn't sure what to expect but I was willing to try and conquer my fears. My fears were many. Would the physical pain overwhelm me? Would the end result find me living in another dungeon of depression? I wondered if my spiritual family would accept me again. I also feared the choice I had made may have been too radical; because I was stubborn, I may become worse off. I had left a sturdy shelter, a soft bed, and a refrigerator full of food. Yet, these things were chains, and I was ready to break free. Eventually, I made it to West Tennessee.

It was an awkward feeling, coming back into a town who just a few months back gave me a hero's welcome. That night I set up camp at Chickasaw State Park. I didn't sleep well, and I was the only one camping in the park. I can remember having fears of wild animals creeping into my camp and attacking. My anxieties were high, but I made it through the night, thanks to prescription drugs. The morning soon came. I woke with very little sleep. I was tired, in pain, and going to work seemed dreadful, but I was there to get better. I called Mike, and within a few hours, I was hard at it out on the farm, hauling trees, cutting grass, moving bees and getting stung numerous times. I shoveled manure; by the sweat of my brow, I was regaining all that I once felt was lost. I dug trenches. I cut timber. I swallowed my pride. No job was below me. I labored day in and day out. By the sweat of my brow, I did everything a farm hand could do. I was, if anything, humbled.

Day in and day out, I worked hard and long. Eventually, I walked into the small country churches of Pinson and Jacks Creek. Both places did as they always did before and welcomed me with warm open arms. Little by little, I was weaning myself off the drugs. Little by little, I was gaining strength within my entire being. My physical body was being toughened. My mental anxieties were lessening, but most importantly, my spiritual being was being renewed. The clouds were parting and the sun was beginning to shine again. I saw a bright future. I saw myself coming through another one of life's valleys, yet, still there were so many uncertainties. So, like so many times before, I decided to take another leap of faith. It was time to share my story, and I couldn't think of any better way than through a walk about.

Just four years prior, I had hitch-hiked across country for twenty-nine days. I swore I would never repeat that journey, but life had brought me to another cross-road. Against all odds and common sense, I decided to do a forty day/forty night hitch-hike across America. Was this a wise choice? Well, the juice gets better…

## *The Road Home: Desperado*

'They' say, "When the going gets tough, the tough get going." God had brought me through so much, His spirit was being revamped into my blood, and through His blood I was ready to move mountains. I began making preparations. I gave Mike a two week notice. I got in touch with my California and Alaskan connections, and said I would be headed that way soon, by way of thumb. I contacted my old college and decided to finish my teaching license once I returned. I saved up and bought a video camera. I sent messages out all over the internet about the journey. The responses were overwhelming and varied:

"Do you ever stop?"... "Jeremy, see ya when ya get here?"... "Sounds like fun!"... "I think you should think twice about this."... "If you make it here, you got a home waiting." "Where will you sleep?"..."Jeremy, we love you."... "Haven't you already made this journey?" All these responses and many more filled my mind, but I was determined and inspired. Inspired by God's power and by a specific quote, I was ready to take on the road. God's spirit was moving within me and this quote replayed over and over in my head. I first heard it in the film Coach Carter. In this movie a young man comes to a crossroad; his coach had loved him with the right kind of love, and had questioned him repeatedly, "What is your deepest fear?" The player had seemingly lost everything but his coach and his team, and despite the odds, he was not a quitter. He quotes Marrianne Williamson and it moved me:

*"Our deepest fear is not that we are inadequate. Our deepest fear is that we are powerful beyond measure. It is our light, not our darkness that most frightens us. We ask ourselves, who am I to be brilliant, gorgeous, talented, fabulous? Actually, who are you not to be? You are a child of God. Your playing small does not serve the world. There is nothing enlightened about shrinking so that other people won't feel insecure around you. We are all meant to shine, as children do. We were born to make manifest the glory of God that is within us. It's not just in some of us; it's in everyone. And as we let our own light shine, we unconsciously give other people permission to do the same. As we are liberated from our own fear, our presence automatically liberates others."*

To these people I said: "No, I will not stop. I will see you if I get there. Life is fun! Think twice? No, I have thought about this a thousand times. Thanks for inviting me; I hope we can visit. I will sleep where the Lord leads me. I love you too. No, a man can never make the same journey twice. A man grows, a man changes, and with him so does time and so do the seasons. Every journey has its own purpose." To me and my mind, this journey would prove that with God, man can overcome any obstacle. This journey would heal the scars hidden within. This journey was devoted to my team and my coach. All I had to do was not shrink and let my light shine.

I sent one last internet message out before departing. I asked that if anyone would like to help me, there were several ways to do so. One, they could send me a CD to listen to. Two, they could write me letters to read along the way. I stated, "It gets lonely out on the road." Third, I asked for prayers. Of all the people who seemed interested, only a few followed through. In fact, of all the people who stated they would do something only a few stand out. Nancy Bogue bought me a new pair of shoes. Mike gave me a few extra dollars. Cris Bodily, my childhood friend, made me a CD. Kevin Youngblood prayed specifically for my journey to glorify God, as did the Jacks Creek congregation. I'm sure that many prayers were sent up on my behalf. I am sure that many people wanted to mail me letters, but of all those who said they would do so, only one package came. It was from a lady I had long been friends with, Bethany Odom. I hadn't seen her in years, but she had always been a good friend to me and kept in touch. Also, she did something that is really kind of hard to do: she impressed me.

I opened the package and inside was several letters. Each had a certain day to be read. There was a mystery package to be opened on day twenty. There were two CD's and a black, leather bound journal. When I opened, it read, "Jeremy, I hope this journal helps you along your journey. Be safe--- Me." Then, in small writing inscribed at the bottom was these words "James 4:13-15/ Carpe Diem" I had heard both before but didn't remember either. The scripture from James reads, "Now listen, you who say, today or tomorrow we will go to this or that city, spend a year there, carry on business and make money." Why, you do not even know what will happen tomorrow. What is your life? You are a mist that appears for a little while and then vanishes. Instead, you ought to say, "If it is the Lord's will, we will live and do this or that."

At first I was confused, but then when I looked up Carpe Diem everything fit perfectly; Carpe Diem is Latin for "Cease the Day." Bethany was a great encourager, and she had followed through. As I packed my bag to begin my own journey, she was flying over me, headed east to cease her own day in Cambodia. She was going to teach photography and share God's love. I admit, after receiving that package a new crush was formed (Bethany, hope you're not blushing). For years I had been looking for the 'one.' And for a split moment, I thought, "Could it possibly be her?" My mental response, "Most likely not, the love of a woman was not in my future. I had so many failed relationships, so many red flags. I was divorced, a recovering drug addict, and I was over-weight, tattooed and scarred from head to toe." To add to all these attractive qualities, I was an impulsive, unstructured, rolling stone, without a home. In short, I was a hopeless romantic. These thoughts were my truths, and I was willing to accept them. Plus, I still had feelings for Ally. I thought, "Love may come, but it was inevitable love would always leave. Yet naturally, I stuck with the motto, "It never hurts to flirt." And with that thought, I moved forward.

The next few days I packed and repacked my bag

at my granny Patty's house. I did so in the basement. Mentally and spiritually preparing for this trip was a rough roller coaster. I made a small wooden cross to signify my faith. I had a small American flag to signify my patriotism. I packed a Bible, a CD player and some CD's. For food, I packed tuna, peanut butter, tortillas and a fishing pole with lures. For fluids, I had a gallon of water and a two-liter camel pack to refill. For survival purposes and hygiene, I packed two changes of clothing, lots of socks and underwear, one bar of soap, a towel and rag, deodorant, toothpaste and a tooth-brush, a poncho, sleeping bag, a few knives, a tent, flash light, batteries, two video cameras and some lighters.

Packing all this stuff, I thought about the first hitch-hiking trip. I had done this before but with less. I was also younger, in better shape, and without traumatic injuries. As I picked up the bag and strapped it to my back, I thought, "Jeremy, this is stupid." My pride and my senses collided. I wanted so badly to hide away. Too many people knew and I had so many doubts. I wanted to back out. Nevertheless, in the face of adversity, and not wanting to deal with the humility, I walked against the wind. I looked around at what used to be the dungeon of depression. I remembered my purpose. I had come so far and had many cheering me on. I simply could not quit. My life had meaning and my story had to be shared. So, I took a deep breath and prayed. The dungeon of depression had no more hold on my life. With nearly seventy pounds strapped to my once broken back, I went upstairs to meet my mom and grandmother. Granny handed me eighty dollars and Mom took me to the interstate. I hugged them both, and before the morning sun could heat the June pavement, I was headed out on another journey. My friends, can you feel it? Can you taste it? Are you thirsty? Would you like a little juice?

## *The Road Home: The Enlightenment*

Stepping out on the highway that hot June morning did more than anyone could ever understand. All I can say is that the choice to do so liberated me, my life, and my soul. I can recall my exact thoughts. I was alive! I was walking and breathing. Yeah, I was hurt but pain is only temporary. It seemed all my life death was chasing me. Death will certainly get us all. I had buried friends and relatives, young and old. The fondest of them was my daughter Laila Lynn. So many times, I had confronted death, and so many times I had begged to live another day. After numerous car wrecks, overdoses, slips and falls, God had always protected me. For goodness sakes, I had at one moment been inside an elephant's mouth and trampled on by four ten-thousand pound animals. Yet, I was alive.

Many may think that taking this trip was idiotic. At first, I questioned the rationale of such a bold choice. However, not to take the trip would have been the death of me. I didn't have a home I could call my own. I didn't own my car. I was swamped with student loans; in fact, I had nothing but debt. Yet, I was not worried about anything but one debt in particular at this point in life. It is a debt I know I will never be able to repay: the debt paid by Christ. After the elephant attack, I could no longer deny that miracles still happen. I was a walking testimony of God's incomprehensible love. I was a citizen of the greatest nation in human history and I could without fear share this with all my fellow Americans. I might be materially poor, but I am greatly blessed in riches from above. I am free and able to share these heavenly riches with all my fellow Americans and it is my duty to do so. And so, it is here at this point in the story I give you the juice:

Elephant Juice: What is it? Simply put, it is love. Not love like you or I understand it, but a love known as agape. If you were to sit across a room from somebody and without sound you mouthed the words "elephant juice," the person reading your lips may at first, squint his or her eyes as to say, "I don't understand." However, by the second or third time they read your lips, they would understand you to say, "I love you." Agape has several definitions, but the original use of this word can be defined as the love God has for humankind. It is an unselfish love without limitations and I am deeply grateful to share it with you. I am honored to have a life that shows His redemption, and though I can't repay that debt given on the cross, I can pay tribute to the king. This king long ago gave his blood for me. His blood fills many jars and is offered for every person on this planet. His life stopped time and started time. The juice is the blood, and in the blood is life, no doubt about it. Still have doubts? Let me finish the story.

For forty days and forty nights, I traveled from Nashville, Tennessee, to Mobile, Alabama. From Mobile to Oxford, Mississippi, from Oxford to Memphis, Tennessee, from Memphis to Little Rock, Arkansas, from Little Rock to Piedmont, Missouri, from Piedmont to Oklahoma City, from Oklahoma City to Houston, Texas, from Houston back to Oklahoma City, from Oklahoma City, to Davidson, North Carolina, from Davidson to Clemson, South Carolina, From Clemson into Georgia, and from there I landed back to Nashville, Tennessee. What happen during those forty days? Well, I did what God showed me to do. I just lived on His love. I cannot express it any better than the word itself':

*"The Son radiates God's own glory and expresses the very character of God, and he **sustains everything** by the mighty power of his command. When he had cleansed us from our sins, he sat down in the place of honor at the right hand of the majestic God in heaven."* Hebrews 1:3

In Alabama I made new friends with those who picked up the lone drifter, and I shared my story with them. One such person was Chris Ierubino and son Pierce. I visited friends and churches that helped me when I was trapped in the Bangkok hospital. I was able share a day or two with some friends from my Europe trip, Amanda and Ragan. I went into Mississippi and stayed with a man named Cason and his wife Casey. They too have always shared God's love with me. On July fourth, I watched fireworks in Memphis, Tennessee with people who at first I saw as strangers and now I call them friends. Once in Arkansas, I sought out and found Mikeal 'Goose' Gossage. I spent a week with him and his wife.

During that week, we went to Petite Jean State Park and played in the waterfalls. I was able to contact Bethany, and I thanked her for being my friend and tried my hardest to woo her with my charm. The crush intensified. In fact, I showed Mikeal a picture of her and said, "This lady here would be perfect for me." Later that week Mikeal and I climbed Pinnacle Mountain. We prayed together. Mikeal knew I was lonely and seeking a true spiritual mate, but the reality of my situation left me thinking it would never happen. From Mikeal's home, I went to the Privett farm in Piedmont, Missouri. There I was able to work and make some cash. They gave me more than I deserved.

Then, the next thing I knew, I was eating fancy Italian meals in Oklahoma with a good friend named Becca. She dropped me off outside of Tahlequah, and from there I made my way to Oklahoma City and shared more of my story with others who just wanted to pick up the man walking down the road. Carl was one such character. Once in Oklahoma City, I was eager to visit the Gates of Time and the Survivor Tree.

In 1995 America was attacked from the inside. As I was sitting there looking into the reflecting pool and imagining how violent our world is, tears of confusion and sympathy formed. I thought, "Here I stand where many died; innocent lives from the beginning of this country were moved west on a trail of tears and at the end of that trail a pool of tears remains. Life is so damn hard. How can God allow such a thing? In fact, I questioned, "God, are you really there?" Then, as I looked around the corner, I saw two children playing in the memorial, and I saw life and the meaning of the survivor tree. For a second, I doubted God, but then when I saw the love that conquered the pain, I knew He was there. God says we are to love as children and seeing those children playing where tragedy had struck brought hope back into my heart, and that was all I needed to carry on.

I strapped on my bag and decided to head south. I was supposed to catch a ride up into Kansas for my friend's wedding, but God had other plans. I walked all day in the sun until blisters formed on every toe and on both heels. It was over a hundred-degrees and with each step a yelp of pain sounded from my sun burnt face. "Oh, oh, AHHH!!" It was intense, and I was ready to give up. I had been gone for 30 days, and ten more seemed too much. I was looking for the nearest bush and shade. Then, as I looked down the highway, a white pick-up was reversing my way. Well, we have all heard that everything happens for a reason. It is my strong belief that God put me in a place where I was most needed. He had closed some doors and opened others. I was not supposed to make that wedding; instead, I was supposed to make friends with Carlos.

Due to legality issues, I can't go much into detail about Carlos, but you are welcome to read between the lines. Carlos was the most exciting and intimidating of all the rides. Yet, he loved the drifter. Carlos not only fed and entertained me, but he also befriended me. We made a deal. If I would drive him to Houston so he could 'pay' to get his cousin back, he would buy me a ticket to anywhere in the United States I wished to go. He was drunk and it was my duty to keep the roads as safe as possible. Carlos, I know not if you ever will read this, but if you happen to pick this book up, know that I love you and respect you. I only pray you find that God who you said sent me to you.

I ended up spending three days with Carlos. I met his whole family and we had a fiesta. After one good night sleep he asked me where I wanted to go, and after some deep thinking, it was obvious; I needed to go and see Nolan, the man who encouraged me years ago that I could do anything. So, Carlos bought me a ticket to Davidson, North Carolina, and I met up with my old pal. We fished and scuba'd and just chilled by the water. It was refreshing to say the least. Eventually, I headed south into South Carolina and Georgia where I finished my 40 day, 40 night trip. I shared my story one last time with the Tannery family, who I had long been friends with. They put me up in a cabin on a crystal clear stream. They loved and fed me. I hadn't seen them in over sixteen years, but it was like it had always been before. We were family, and were so happy to be together. They even threw me a party, and of all the conversations that took place, one stood out the most.

Tim an older and wiser man seemed sincerely interested in my life. He asked me the question I had been asking myself for quite some time. "Jeremy, what do you want out of life?" My answer was simple, "I want a wife and children of my own. I would like to be a best selling author and use the money to do mission work for God and travel the world. I don't care about having a big fancy home or nice vehicles; I just want the love of a woman who is right for me and children to hold and rear with the love of the father." Tim said something that changed my life and my attitude. I hear one can speak things into existence. Tim said boldly, "You're going to get it, Jeremy." I said, "You think so?" Without doubt Tim said, "I know it." He believed and I believed him. He had little doubt and I had many. Yet, I do know God answers prayers, and so I continued praying for a wife and children.

## *The Road Home: God Answers Prayers*

I returned to Tennessee a changed man. The elephant attack had finally ended. Sure, I still have some pain, but that's life, right? Without trials we cannot grow; without pain heaven has no purpose. I want heaven, and I am greatly blessed to have had so many trials and tribulations in my first thirty years of life. And once I embraced the hard times as blessings, I realized I needed to turn these blessings to praise, and the neatest thing of the whole story is that the juice gets even better.

I ended up back at work on the bee farm and picked up odd jobs here and there. I signed up for a few more classes to help me reach my educational goals as a licensed teacher. I moved into a little humble home and started living life. I also began substituting at all grade levels. I was not completely back on top, but I was close. The one thing I felt I needed more than anything was a partner. I began praying, "God, please send me a wife, a helper, and a friend. I'm lonely and it is not good for man to be alone."

I began playing the field, and to my surprise, I had a few ladies responding. Even my dear friend Ally came back into the picture, and so did some of those wrong ladies I had always been accustomed to chasing. Adding to the mix was Bethany Odom. She had made it back from Cambodia. I practically begged her to meet me, and she d every time. Ally and I eventually had a date. I ... ner out for her birthday. It was nice reuniting with her. Also, I looked up Samantha my romantic partner from my first book. She had never left my thoughts, but no woman seemed to fit. Nothing seemed concrete. However, I did notice I was happy again, and I had started writing this book; I had no idea how much would change in the progression of writing it, but God's love made the juice even sweeter.

Every first Wednesday night of each month I visit the Church of Pinson, Tennessee. They have a singing fellowship and a fellowship dinner afterward. It's one of my favorite things to do. Not only do I get food for my body, but I also get the bread of life fed to my soul. There in the church is one of the most significant mentors of my life, Donald Taylor. Don was the leader of the Belgium group that first changed my life. I saw his happiness and knew I wanted that same joy. He was happy because of the joy the Lord had given him. It was a sincere happiness. It was not a happiness that came from material things, but a happiness that came from the spirit of God, a happiness that never fails to show itself. I was hungry for it, and he gently took me under his wing along with a few others. On this particular Wednesday night, a change occurred. I learned a little more about prayer life.

The teaching this night came from the Old Testament. A woman in the book of Kings had lost her husband and owed tribute to the king. She summoned up the prophet of God and asked for help. He, in turn, asked her what she had to pay this debt, and she replied, "All I have is this jar of oil." The prophet of God tells her to go and gather more jars. He said gather jars from everyone. And so, the woman set out about the town asking for the jars of her neighbors and her neighbors' neighbors. The lady gathered a large number of jars. Then, she summoned up the prophet. With one small of jar of oil, God was able to fill every jar she collected with oil. She not only was able to pay her debt, but she had enough to live on for the rest of her life.

This lesson teaches us that God is mighty and merciful. With faith He can do all things and answer every prayer. He wants us to be happy, but sometimes we must have real, genuine faith and we got to bring our jars before him. He wants us to have a real personal relationship with Him, just as we would with any other person we love, but more than that, He wants us to allow Him to bless us and be specific in our prayers. We all ask in times of need, but sometimes we don't ask enough, and we don't bring enough jars and we don't bring our all. It seems we pray with mediocre expectations. We figure God knows what we need, so, why ask? Why hit our knees? Well, I knew one thing for sure that Wednesday night; I had not brought all my jars to God. I had been growing. My life had been changing, and through the trials He had continually showed His grace and love to me. Nevertheless, that night after the lesson, I changed my prayer life. I went home and hit my knees and begin bringing all my jars to him. My prayers went from, "God I need a wife and kids," to a prayer like this:

"Father, oh gracious father, I know you hear me. I know you are there, and I know you want to fill my jars, so tonight I'm going to bring all my jars before you. God,

I am now approaching thirty-two, and my first jar is that I not only want a wife, but I want a young, beautiful, 'Christian' wife who wants to have children, travel the world, and do missions for your kingdom. God, I want a wife who wants to adopt kids who are without. God, I also want to share my story with the world and be a best selling author, but first, I want a wife. And God, my next jar I want you to fill, and I know you can fill it, is that I want these things now. I am tired of waiting, so if you will, I ask you to bring this woman, whoever she may be, into my life. God I pray this with faith. And, I ask you to fill one more jar; make it obvious. Thank you for hearing my cries, In Christ name I pray these things, Amen."

I began praying this prayer on September 1st 2009. On September 23rd I got a text from Bethany Odom. It simply said, "I miss talking to you." I called her immediately and again begged her to come meet me; we agreed to meet half way. She would come and be the photographer at my brother's wedding. God had spun those infinite revolving doors and all things lined up. She and I had our first date on September 26th at a redneck wedding. That very night we were engaged. Two weeks later we were married by Mikeal 'Goose' Gossage on top of Pinnacle Mountain in Arkansas, the same mountain Mikeal and I had climbed on my forty day-forty night trip. I cry now thinking of how beautifully God has blessed me. And to make things even greater, to make the juice even sweeter, we are now going to have a child. A month after we were married Bethany got pregnant. My first born son is soon to come, his name, Journey Abel McGill. With tears of joy I say, PRAISE BE TO GOD! He is my all in all.

## *Concluding Remarks:*

## *The 'Journey' Continues*

Dear reader, I hope you have enjoyed this little story. I appreciate your time and your being part of my life. It is my prayer that you, too, find that peace that is offered from the one, true father and that you begin to bring your jars before him. He will fill them, maybe not the way you see it, but in a much greater way. God loves you regardless of your circumstance; no one is too far for God's grace to reach; in fact, He is there with open arms waiting for you today: He stands on the stormy seas and calms the sea for you. All one needs is faith. Remember Psalm 23, written by David a murderous, adulterous man who was considered to be a man after God's on heart. His Psalm reads:

"The LORD is my shepherd, I shall not want. He makes me lie down in green pastures, he leads me beside quiet waters, he restores my soul. He guides me in paths of righteousness for his name's sake. Even though I walk through the valley of the shadow of death, I will fear no evil, for you are with me; your rod and your staff, they comfort me. You prepare a table before me in the presence of my enemies. You anoint my head with oil; my cup overflows. Surely goodness and love will follow me all the days of my life, and I will dwell in the house of the LORD forever."

As for my future and my overflowing cup, my wife is indeed young and beautiful. She is ten years my younger and wants to serve God through missions. Her God-given talent is photography, and apparently God has given me the gift of writing and teaching. We are each other's perfect mate, and I praise Him for the gift He has given me by bringing Bethany into my life. We hope to serve in every way possible. And as Joshua put it, "As for me and my house, we will serve the Lord."

We hope one day to return to wild elephant valley. I want to find those fourteen men who carried me out of the jungle and thank them personally; so yes, that means there will be possibly be another book, so long as the elephant remembers that I am not that tasty. We would like for God to open a door in Africa; however, we are open to what ever door he decides to open for us. He has already opened one such door and by January 1, 2011 we will be in NYC showing and shining God's love.

We love America, but we love God more, we would like to also start a magazine, and we don't mind asking for your prayers. Pray for us and as we try to pray for all of our people. By purchasing this book you have already helped us in our mission efforts. We are always open to hear from you. We plan to stay in NYC for at least five years. But we also understand our plans and God's plans don't always match up. So, if you would like to, don't hesitate go ahead and contact us. Below are different ways to do so. We want to be a part of your life and most of all we want to see you in heaven when Christ returns, for you, I will come back and take you to be with me that you also may be where I am." – Jesus Christ, The Messiah

## Contact Information:

Jeremy McGill
731-608-5716

Facebook: Jeremy.Mcgill@students.fhu.edu
jmelephantjuice@gmail.com
mcgilladventures.blogspot.com
elephantjuice.us


Ps. remember the man a few pages back who thought he would never have a wife and children of his own? Remember the man who prayed with faith for his jars to be filled?
Turn the page and see how blessed he is, and how God has shined His light once again on a once dead man who rose again...

**Journey Abel McGill born
August 20, 2010.**